More praise for *Lisa Murphy on Being Child Centered*

"Lisa Murphy is challenging us to reflect on what we really believe about children and how we put those beliefs into action. She knows we are ready for the challenge to stand up for children and create the environments they deserve. This book is an indispensable guide for us."
—Heather Bernt-Santy, podcast host of *That Early Childhood Nerd*

"Tender, completely engaging, honest, real, and relevant to the promotion of PLAY. Everyone should put this book in hand and not let it go."
—Daniel Hodgins, author of *Boys: Changing the Classroom, Not the Child* and *Get Over It: Relearning Guidance Practices*

"Lisa writes humorously about real-life teachers and children while challenging us to think seriously and deeply about our everyday experiences with young children. She asks us to provide our children with the gifts of time, play, nature, freedom, autonomy, consistency, relationships, and opportunities. The nine attributes she proposes are indeed the heart and soul—the foundation—of the child-centered early childhood classroom."
—Dr. Laurel Bongiorno, dean, Champlain College, Division of Education & Human Studies

"Very readable and thought-provoking book. . . . This very timely book is a must read for everyone at every level—from newbies in the field to experienced teachers and policy makers."
—Jenna Bilmes, author of *Beyond Behavior Management*, Second Edition

"*Lisa Murphy on Being Child Centered* is a must-read for anyone interested in creating a child-centered, play-based, relationship-focused early learning environment."
—Jeff Johnson, author of *Babies in the Rain: Promoting Play, Exploration, and Discovery with Infants and Toddlers*

Lisa Murphy on Being Child Centered

Other Redleaf Press books by Lisa Murphy

Even More Fizzle, Bubble, Pop & Wow!
Simple Science Experiments for Young Children

Lisa Murphy on Play: The Foundation of Children's Learning

Ooey Gooey Handbook: Identifying and Creating
Child-Centered Environments

Ooey Gooey Tooey: 140 Exciting Hands-On
Activity Ideas for Young Children

Lisa Murphy on
BEING CHILD CENTERED

by Lisa Murphy, MEd

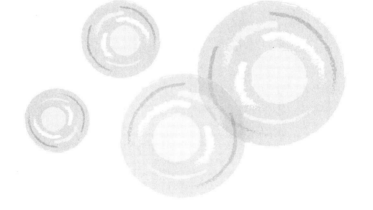

Redleaf Press®
www.redleafpress.org
800-423-8309

Published by Redleaf Press
10 Yorkton Court
St. Paul, MN 55117
www.redleafpress.org

First edition 2019
Senior editor: Heidi Hogg
Managing editor: Douglas Schmitz
Cover design: Renee Hammes and Charles Rue Woods
Cover photograph by Laura Olivas/Moment/via Getty Images
Interior design by Louise OFarrell
Image on page 19 designed by Todd Rohnke

Characteristics of play on pages 7–8 excerpted from "Definitions of Play" by Peter Gray, *Scholarpedia*, www.scholarpedia.org/article/Definitions_of_Play. Reprinted with permission.

Why do children climb on pages 74–75 adapted from *The Developmental Benefits of Playgrounds* by Joe L. Frost, Pei-San Brown, John A. Sutterby, and Candra D. Thornton, Washington DC: Association for Childhood Education International, © 2004. Reprinted with permission.

Play types on pages 178–185 adapted from *A Playworker's Taxonomy of Play Types* by Bob Hughes, London: Playlink, © 2002 and *Play Types* by Play Wales, Cardiff: Play Wales, © 2017. Reprinted with permission.

Typeset in Adobe Chaparral Pro
Printed in the United States of America

26 25 24 23 22 21 20 19   1 2 3 4 5 6 7 8

Library of Congress Cataloging-in-Publication Data
Names: Murphy, Lisa, M.Ed. author.
Title: Lisa Murphy on being child centered / by Lisa Murphy.
Description: First edition. | St. Paul, MN : Redleaf Press, 2019. |
   Includes bibliographical references. | Summary: "This work provides an in-depth exploration of Lisa Murphy's approach to working with children. The author outlines nine attributes programs need to build an environment that's child centered, where play, developmentally appropriate practice, and academic standards all come together under one roof. Using true-to-life examples, anecdotes, and her signature conversational style, this book presents and explores the true identifying attributes of a hands-on, play-based, child-centered environment"— Provided by publisher.
Identifiers: LCCN 2019027891 (print) | LCCN 2019027892 (ebook) | ISBN
   9781605546155 (paperback) | ISBN 9781605546162 (ebook)
Subjects: LCSH: Play. | Early childhood education. | Child development.
Classification: LCC LB1139.35.P55 M86 2019 (print) | LCC LB1139.35.P55
   (ebook) | DDC 372.21—dc23
LC record available at https://lccn.loc.gov/2019027891
LC ebook record available at https://lccn.loc.gov/2019027892

Printed on acid-free paper

It is not about play eliminating order, it's about letting play flourish and thus optimizing order by minimizing it.

—Shepherd Siegel, PhD, author of *Disruptive Play: The Trickster in Politics and Culture*

Contents

Acknowledgments

It is with heartfelt sincerity and gratitude that I tip my hat to those who assisted during this labor of love. First and foremost, to the UNCondo Crew, the ECE Nerd Collective, and the hive-mind that is social media. All y'all provided support and feedback when I needed input from *people*, not just the results of a Google search. To those of you who tolerated my habit of processing ideas out loud, talking to an invisible audience that was for no one's benefit but my own as well as those of you who offered opportunities for interactive banter and dialogue. To my muse. You crazy thirsty beeyatch, I knew you didn't abandon me, but you scared me there for a minute. Thank you for coming back. Now get outta here, I'll let you know when I need you again. To PJ. Our story is just beginning, but I still want to acknowledge your role in supporting me at all stages of the entire process, especially when I thought my muse flew the coop. I am forever thankful for the space she and I came to call *home* as we pushed through and brought this bad boy to completion. To Kane. For making sure I left the house occasionally for a nice long walk to give my brain a break and for sitting under the table at my feet offering that silent kind of support that only a dog can provide. To the eagles who cried out both a morning and an evening alarm. And finally, last but certainly not least, to all the friends and family members I have not seen in what feels like forever. I cannot thank you enough for your ongoing patience as I put my nose to the grindstone in my efforts to give birth to book five.

I owe all y'all a killer Taco Tuesday.

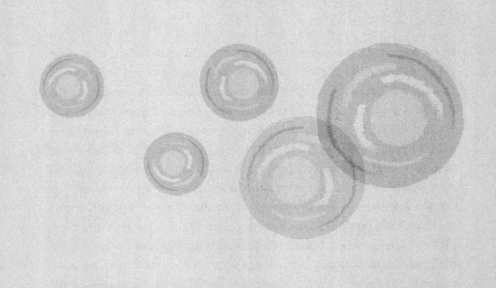

PART 1

Why Did I Write This Book?

HEY THERE! Whether you are new to the party and not familiar with me at all or a card-carrying, self-proclaimed groupie, I welcome you to my new book! I am very excited to share it with you, as it's been bouncing around in my brain for a while now, just waiting for the best time to pop out. Truth be told, my muse got a little stubborn during the process, and for a moment I thought she might've called it quits, so I let her rest (or do whatever it is muses do when they abandon their writers) and told myself to be ready when she came back. Which she did, in full force, about three months later. And now we have this, my new baby! Full disclosure: I've never had a *real* baby (that's my sister's department—she has babies, two sets of identical twins, mind you—I have *books*, but I digress), but I think a case can be made as to how the two are *kind of* similar. Especially the gestation part. This idea has been in my head for years! Then it took months to push it all out! But then, finally, after all the work, the complications, the anticipation, the weight gain, the aching back and sleepless nights, it arrived! It's here! *Why hello and welcome, new wee baby book!*

So let's get right to it: some of you are accustomed to my writing style, and some of you are not. But don't worry, you'll figure it out pretty quick. I try to write as though I am talking to you, so for me, this is a two-hundred-page (give or take) conversation. And I'd like to kick-start that conversation by giving you some perspective as to how I arrived at the place of writing the book that you have (thank you!) decided to read.

This book is not my first (it's my fifth!). I'm sure all authors are different, but for me, when I realize there is more to say about an idea or a concept, it might be time to write another book. When there is new information or data or research that supports (or negates!) a position, it might be time. When I notice that an existing idea has more depth than originally thought, it might be time. When folks start asking for one, it might be time too! This book is a combination of all of these things.

In my last book, *Lisa Murphy on Play*, I wrote about and explored in depth how having ongoing opportunities to create, move, sing, discuss, observe, read, and play (what I have come to call *the seven things*) makes a strong foundation that supports the house of higher learning. Inside this house of higher learning are all of the reading, writing, math, science, social studies (read: *academic*) expectations we have for children. The expectations themselves are not the problem; everyone wants children to eventually know how to read, write, understand how things work, spell, do math. The problem is that many of you reading this book are feeling pressure (whether actual or perceived) to begin building the house before the foundation.

In the *Play* book, I reassure readers that when children are provided daily opportunities to do the seven things, they are doing everything they need to "get ready" for school. Additionally, I make a case for *play* being not a separate seventh thing, but rather the *cement* that holds the entire *foundation* together.

Want a huge academic mansion? Then pay attention to the foundation. If the foundation is strong, the house will be too. To keep the house/foundation metaphor going (it really does make sense if you think about it), I'd like to invite you to think of this new book as the philosophical orientation that will guide us as we frame the foundation that supports the house. A philosophical compass, so to speak, that will help us keep our eyes set on true north and guide us, whether we're orienting ourselves for the first time (like building a new child care program from the ground up) or reorienting ourselves after realizing we've drifted philosophically (that we've developed some not very developmentally appropriate habits and are ready to change). My vision is one of creating play-based, child-centered environments, but we need a clear philosophical orientation to remain consistent, focused, and headed in the right direction, so that is what I am offering you here: **nine attributes of being child centered to guide us philosophically as we do just that.**

Why do we need this? Because when you use the phrase *child centered*, too many people envision children running around naked with paint flying through the air, like *Lord of the Flies* is being filmed in the toddler room. Embracing a child-centered philosophy does not mean children do whatever they want, while frazzled adults follow behind and clean up the mess. It is not chaos nor is it anarchy. Being truly child centered is the hardest way to be. It takes a level of passion, dedication, flexibility, and commitment that many have long discarded. Child-centered environments have boundaries, consistency, and expectations. The only thing missing in a child-centered space is an adult's need to control the children. But as per usual, I am getting ahead of myself. And while I will spend the majority of the book outlining and exploring the nine philosophical attributes of being child centered, there are three additional considerations that require our attention first.

First, while the foundation of our house consists of making time each day to create, move, sing, discuss, observe, and read, with play serving as the metaphorical cement holding it all together, what if these things are not being done in a *developmentally appropriate* fashion?

Second, what do we mean by *play* anyway?

And third, what good is it if we advocate for play and insist on being developmentally appropriate but are neglecting *relationships*? You can call yourself play based all day long, but by overlooking the interconnection between everyone in the program, adults and children alike, a huge part of what makes a program a *good* program is missing. That might sound harsh, but it is 100 percent true. It does not matter how playful your program is, or what kind of developmentally appropriate activities are on your lesson plan, or how "accredited" you are, or how many "stars" the program has if, in fact, no one takes into consideration that David's dog died over the weekend, Elizabeth didn't get enough sleep last night, Rowan's shoes are too tight, Oliver has a brand-new baby brother, or that the "behavior problem" you think is Nathan is actually the result of watching a family fight turn into mommy getting arrested. Again.

Being developmentally appropriate, and understanding how play and best practice and relationships are all interconnected, are vital parts of a child-centered philosophy.

Please permit a relevant backstory: Over the years I have learned that when you share ideas, they often become better ideas. When you put a handful of like-minded wizards in the same room talking about things they are passionate about, there's a strong chance that, with their input, your little idea might start growing into a full-blown idea, and that's what happened to me while attending a conference a couple of years ago. I found myself smack in the middle of a very engaging and spontaneous conversation about how Peter Gray's five characteristics of play, developmentally appropriate practice (DAP), and Abraham Maslow's hierarchy of needs *fit* within the frame/foundation/house model that I explore in the *Play* book. We were talking about it, drawing diagrams to try to show what it might look like. We had houses, triangles and squares and circles taped up on the walls as we attempted to create some kind of visual representation of the words we were kicking around. While this was all happening, I realized it was *not* going to be enough to simply explore nine philosophical attributes in the new book; I was going to need to explore these elements as well.

Now let's be real, exploring play theory or the full framework of developmentally appropriate practice or the contributions of Abraham

Maslow are major topics in and of themselves. Entire books and college courses are dedicated to each of them individually, so it goes without saying that this is not the forum for an in-depth exploration of them. *However*, without minimizing their significance or glossing over their importance, what I *do* want to do at this juncture is provide a general overview of the three things we were kicking around at that conference—developmentally appropriate practice (DAP), Abraham Maslow's hierarchy of needs, and Peter Gray's characteristics of play—in an effort not only to keep the conversation going but to show why we cannot afford to ignore their influence as we deepen our understanding of what it means to be child centered.

Developmentally Appropriate Practice

In the mid-1980s the National Association for the Education of Young Children (NAEYC) decided it was time to specifically define what was meant by the phrase "being developmentally appropriate," so in 1986 they issued a formal position statement, and then in 1987 they published a book that outlined what a developmentally appropriate program looks like. The book was revised in 1997 and again in 2009. At the core of the theory of DAP is a belief that we must know about child development and how children learn, we must be familiar with general ages and stages, and we also must know what is both individually and culturally appropriate. We must also make sure that our activities, planning, and programming meet all four developmental domains: cognitive development, language and literacy development, physical development, and social-emotional development. A concern shared by many practitioners (myself included) is that for too long we have focused only on children's cognitive and language and literacy development, at the expense of their physical and social-emotional development. Consequently, the early childhood experience that many children receive is grossly out of balance.

If we ignore one domain at the expense of another, we are no longer being developmentally appropriate. Overlooking cognitive development in the name of *play* is just as "not OK" as overlooking social-emotional development in the name of *readiness*. One is *not* more important than the other! Because social-emotional and physical development have been ignored for so long, these two areas might require specific targeted interventions, but that does *not* mean we downplay or ignore language and literacy and cognitive development. Does this make sense? All four developmental domains are weighted equally. A "good program" is paying attention to all of them. Being child centered and DAP go hand in hand.

Maslow's Hierarchy of Needs

Abraham Maslow (1908–1970) was an American psychologist most famous for his hierarchy of needs; many of you are probably familiar with the iconic image of a pyramid used to visually represent this idea. Basic needs such as food, shelter, clothing are at the bottom, and self-actualization is at the top. We cannot move up until the need below has been met. Maslow contributed more to the field of psychology than a simple image of a pyramid, but for those of us in early childhood education, this is the part of his work that very much resonates with ours.

What is so beautifully truthful and frustrating about this hierarchy is that within the course of a day, depending on the day you're having, you could be bouncing up and down it all day long. I often compare the top of the pyramid (self-actualization) to a really good program, a really fantastic lesson plan, or even a very strong teaching staff . . . none of which matter a hill o' beans if teachers are not taking into consideration modifications that must be made when children show up hungry, feel tired, are distracted by an itchy tag on the inside of their shirt, or are confused because they don't know who is picking them up after school today.

Our ability to meet the needs of children requires us to know what those needs are, both in general (read: knowledge of child development) and individually, which means paying attention to this child in front of me, right here and right now, and remembering that the relationship I cultivate with her is crucial to her development. This means there might be occasions when I put my adult agenda on pause since tending to tears is more important than snack being on time; we must be mindful of never missing an opportunity to strengthen relationships. Even if this means being "off schedule." We aren't off schedule because we are shirking our duties or responsibilities, but because we realize it doesn't matter what we thought we *should* be doing—the children are showing us what *needs* to be done. People guided by a child-centered philosophy are able to see the difference.

The Five Characteristics of Play

Dr. Peter Gray, author of *Free to Learn* who graciously granted permission for me to include this material here for you, has identified five characteristics of play. But before we get to them, Gray states that there are three general points to consider when thinking about play: First, play has to do with motivation and attitude, not necessarily a specific behavior. Meaning you could be a part of a baseball game that doesn't feel like play and later be pounding nails or doing yard work that very much does. It's about one's attitude toward the behavior.

Second, play isn't all or nothing. Children can be 100 percent engaged in what we might call "pure play" and adults might bring a *playful spirit* (a percentage of playfulness, if you will) to whatever the task is at hand. Of course there is no tool to measure the percentage of play someone brings to an activity or task, so Gray offers that we might consider playfulness as a matter of degree.

Third, play has *refused* to be neatly defined ever since researchers began studying it! Play is more of a mash-up, if you will, of many identifiable characteristics. And after reviewing the literature and analyzing many of these previous, existing attempts to define play, Gray thinks the *characteristics* of play can be boiled down to the following five:

1. "Play is self-chosen and self-directed," and the players are always free to quit. If there is no choice, it is not play. Period.

2. "Play is intrinsically motivated—means are more valued than ends." If you are engaged in an activity *only* to reach a specific goal or outcome, it is not play.

3. "Play is guided by mental rules, but the rules leave room for creativity." There is structure to the play and there are rules in the player's minds. Sometimes the rules are spoken, sometimes they aren't; either way, in play there is a self-chosen willingness to behave in accordance to said rules. For example, if you are the "hurt kitty," you need to lie still and "be hurt" until the kitty doctor shows up. To get up and turn into the *dog* without consensus from the other players means you are not only breaking character, you are breaking the mental rules and therefore no longer engaged in play.

4. "Play is imaginative," nonliteral, and marked off in some way from reality. Often referred to as the *paradox of play*, play is serious yet not serious, real and yet not real. While playing, we are in the real world, using blocks, a cape, loose parts, or other props from the real world, yet in some way we are removed from the real world. Sometimes players will say, "Time-out!" to go back to the real world for a drink of water or to move the baby out of the way (or, to expand on the previous characteristic, to ask, HEY! CAN I BE THE DOG NOW?). Calling, "Time-in!" means play has resumed.

5. "Play is conducted in an alert, active, but relatively non-stressed frame of mind." Gray states that this fifth characteristic follows out of the previous four. Some researchers say that when in a true state of play, we are in a "flow" state; our attention is so focused on the activity that our preoccupations with ourselves and of time melt away.

I encourage you to think real hard about these characteristics. I would even go so far as to suggest that any program calling themselves *play based* put themselves through a self-study or an audit of sorts and run their daily routine/expectations/actions/curriculum/program through these criteria to see if they really are indeed *play* based. Not to be a downer, but I bet a lot of what goes on in early childhood settings doesn't even make it past the first characteristic: *that play is self-chosen and self-directed and the players are free to quit at any time.*

If we claim to be advocates of play-based, child-centered environments, it is imperative that we continue to deepen our understanding of how *play* and *learning* live together, not in separate houses.

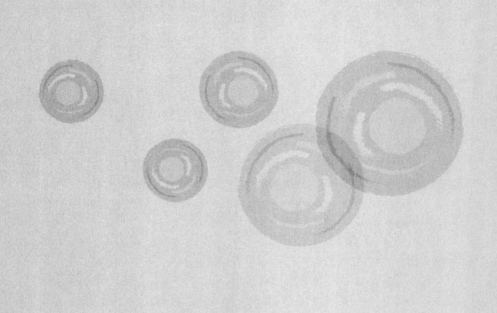

PART 2

Origin of the Nine Philosophical Attributes

I'VE TALKED ABOUT being child centered in workshops and on podcasts, and I even addressed a few of these attributes in the first section of my very first book, *The Ooey Gooey Handbook*. I have a pet peeve about repackaging existing material, but let's be realistic, I wrote that book almost *twenty* years ago!

So for the benefit of you oldies and newbies alike, here's a quick recap of where this all came from: In 1997 when I first started doing workshops, I had *one* outline for *one* single session. I had what I called "The 4Cs"—the initial four **characteristics** of a child-centered environment: (1) children having lots of time, (2) having few restrictions in the space, (3) adults serving as facilitators, and (4) spending lots of time playing outside—and the "3Es" of **ego, environment,** and **experiences**. In this single session I would present the 4Cs and the 3Es, I would share a little bit about Miss Mary and my first day of school, I'd talk a little bit about how when I first started teaching I was paired up with a poopy-face teacher who had lesson plans that were laminated from the 1970s

My company logo was created one afternoon when my art designer at the time (RIP Mr. Zoe) absentmindedly flipped 3E to E3 and doodled the E and 3 into a butterfly. We started talking about butterflies and how they symbolize transformation. I mentioned the depth of transformation that could happen when we, as practitioners, really take the time to examine the 3Es of ego, environment, and experiences . . . and voilà. Ooey Gooey, Inc.'s butterfly logo was born.

(no exaggeration!), we would do some hands-on activities, the participants would have some time to play with the activities I presented, then we'd wrap it up and call it a day.

As time went on, this single workshop session began evolving, changing, and redirecting itself. Before I knew it, new workshop topics were hiving off of the original outline, new articles were written, conversations were happening, and I began refining my content. This first initial workshop session split off into two separate ones, then into three and into four. Before I knew it, my "menu" of workshop topic offerings started to grow considerably. But let's be honest, it's no real secret that I've pretty much been singing the same songs for over twenty years now. My core beliefs have not changed, but what *does* occasionally change is the tune, the timbre, or the tone of how I present them. The main ideas haven't changed, but they get deeper and stronger and, if I may be so bold, *validated*. I owe this to colleagues who continue to stretch and challenge me, books and articles I've read, and all the current research that reinforces the importance of play (read: that proves my point).

In my *Play* book I talk about why I do this work and how my first day of school made a lifelong impact. I tell you about my childhood spent at Mary's Nursery School in Livermore, California, and share with you the starting spot, as it were, of how I got here. In the *The Ooey Gooey Handbook* I tell you about my first day of teaching and how I fell into the abyss with the control-freak, poopy-face laminated ladies. I share with you the insight I gained as I started to crawl my way out with assistance from passionate play-based colleagues and the process of changing my mind. What's my point? That while there is no real reason to rehash those details again here, what I do want to repeat is that *real change takes time, personal growth, and a willingness to be introspective.* And you've got to be willing to do the work!

On my first day of teaching, I *knew* the kind of teacher I wanted to be, but I lacked the language to articulate it. So when I was questioned, I had no words. When I was told to "get with the program" and got put in a time-out (true story) by my poopy-face coteacher, I had no retort. When I was told there wasn't time to play because we had to "get them ready," I knew that was not true, but I had nothing other than a GUT FEELING in my defense. I knew I needed to have more information at my disposal, I needed more ammunition! So I crawled out of the abyss and learned new words. I surrounded myself with people who were further along the path than me. I started doing a lot of thinking, started to change my mind and, more importantly, started to know and understand WHY I was challenging myself to do so in the first place. I started journaling my process. Started keeping track of my questions. Started asking WHY and began rethinking everything I had been taught about teaching. What did I believe in? I asked, "What must be present in a program claiming to be play based and child centered?" and then I set out to find answers. At first I identified three specific attributes, soon after, four, then six, and now nine. Nine philosophical attributes of being child centered.

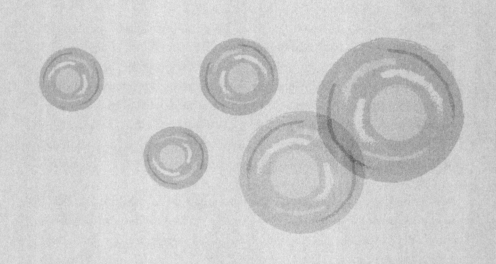

PART 3

What Is Child Centered Anyway?

To MY FELLOW *Princess Bride* fans, I will say, "Lemme 'splain. No. There is too much. Lemme sum up." To the rest of you, I will reiterate the sentiment I shared a few pages back, that being child centered is not chaos. It is not a room filled with screaming children throwing blocks at each other. No. No. No. The philosophical orientation I am describing here is not a thinly veiled preschool version of *The Anarchist Cookbook*, nor is it a Mayhem Manifesto. It *is* about children being able to investigate, play, and explore within a space set up by adults who pay attention to children's needs and interests.

When I first opened my first program, this was a really really really tricky point for early staff members to understand. Many of them had *only* worked in places with unreasonable, developmentally INappropriate expectations of children. And because they had only known employers and programs with rigid and controlling expectations, they didn't really have an understanding of what I was asking of them. Therefore, as could/should/would be expected, after they were hired, their teaching style swung completely in the opposite direction. Why? Because that's what happens before you recalibrate and normalize to a new expectation. They didn't have *any* experience in what I was expecting, so they did the *opposite* of what they had done in the past, thinking that was what I wanted. In a nutshell, it was chaos. It *was* children doing whatever they wanted because the adults weren't sure where the middle ground was between what had previously been expected of them and what I was expecting of them. After too many children being "allowed" to jump off the tables, we regrouped at a staff meeting where I gave them copies of an article I had written about my trip to Amsterdam and how I compared the city to a child-centered program.

The article is called "A Place for Everything and Everything in Its Place," and in it I talk about how immediately upon arriving in Amsterdam, it was obvious that there was a place for everything *but* everything stayed in its place. Want booze? Why not! Beer was cheaper than bottled water! Take Tram 5 to the Leidseplein station and pick your poison. Curious as to the world's oldest profession? Maybe want to peek in the windows? Go to the red-light district (all the trams used to stop there!). Want to partake in a little something-something? Visit one of the coffee shops and no, don't expect a cappuccino. What was my point? If you wanted to partake in any of these activities, they were all there for you. If you didn't, no big deal, but if you *did*, there were designated places for you to go do them. Not once did I see any of these things happening outside of their socially approved quarters, and honestly, I don't think it would've been tolerated if someone tried. It was as though the city had mastered the concept of controlling the environment instead of the inhabitants. The boundaries were clear and consistent, and, because of this, the people moved freely within the established structure. The boundaries were not dependent on someone's mood or whim.

A former professor, the late Barb Chernofsky often said that "children do not test boundaries to make them bigger—they test them to make sure they are still there." When boundaries are always changing, children will keep testing. When boundaries are consistent, children can relax and stop testing. When children see that THIS is the boundary and my MOOD isn't going to change it, they can get down to the business of being children and can spend time investigating, playing, negotiating, and doing other things that come with being a two-year-old, three-year-old, or four-year-old. If a child doesn't know what the boundaries are or if they are always changing willy-nilly or if the teacher's mood du jour determines what is OK and what is not, it can be quite confusing and lead to behavior problems (that aren't really behavior problems). Controlling the environment, instead of the children, is at the core of being child centered. Please remember, being child centered is not permission to let children do whatever they want while you battle a headache, clean up the mess, and fantasize about it being closing time. Deciding to work from a child-centered place is NOT an easy choice. Being child centered is hard. Being play based is hard. It requires endless amounts of understanding, empathy, observation, and a willingness to leave your own ego and issues at the door. It is *easier* to have a daily schedule chopped up into twenty-minute time blocks. It's *easier* to have a fifteen-point rule sheet on the wall. It's *easier* to hide behind excuses about what licensing might or might not allow. It's *easier* to say, "We don't do that here." But it's only easier because it relieves us of the burden of responsibility and the pressure of having to think for ourselves. At this point in my career, and probably yours if you're reading this book, we aren't after *easy*. We are after *meaningful*. And that takes a helluva lot of hard work.

Child-centered spaces are structured, what they are not is *controlling*. As I have already stated, there are boundaries, guidelines, expectations, and adults who are paying attention and acting with intention. The only thing missing is the adult's need to control the children (versus controlling the *environment*). Of course we are going to explore all of this in depth, but I really can't emphasize this piece enough. Exploration of the control piece is crucial as we establish a child-centered environment. Many places claim to be play based, child centered, and developmentally appropriate until we gently start tugging at the control part. As Dan Hodgins has taught so many of us, our goal is to have control *with* and *for* children, not *over* them. This is tricky business for people who have gone into this profession because they like to tell little people what to do.

When I began to actively change my mind as to how I approached teaching, I purposefully began asking question like, "Why do we do this?" I began wondering (not in so many words, but I use the phrase now), "When did I drink that Kool-Aid, and who poured it for me?" At the time I was working in a preschool/child care and still coteaching with Ms. Cynde, my first *real* mentor. She assisted me greatly as I began this inquiry process, gently nudging me constantly with the question that became my initial touchstone: "What is the WORST possible thing that could happen?" I started asking this question all the time and about all the things! Cynde used to joke that I never got in trouble for asking the question, but she would get into trouble just for *thinking* it!

My metaphorical teacher tool belt was gathering more ammunition! I was armed with more than just a belief that "kids learn through play"—I added Cynde's "What is the WORST possible thing that could happen?" question. Then, while attending one of Bev Bos's Good Stuff for Kids conferences, I met Jenny Chapman, who shared with us her visual representation of the Cycle of Change. I'm including it here for two reasons: first, it captures the change process in a very simple, straightforward manner, and second, it works.

One of the things I appreciate the most about her image of change is that it makes room for the process to take as long as it needs to take. Another is that she (like me) encourages you to take one step at a time in order for true reflective changes in our practice to occur. I added Jenny's Cycle of Change to my teacher tool belt. I started reconsidering almost everything I thought to be true in this profession and through the years have shared examples of *my* initial baby steps: how I got rid of my masking tape line-up line, when I started letting the children sit wherever they wanted at circle time, what happened when I stopped saying "One, two, three, eyes on me," when I took the name tags off of the table so the kids could sit wherever they wanted and next to whomever they wanted for snack and lunch. Things that now (hindsight being twenty-twenty) seem like ridiculously small changes but were huge at the time. And here is the point I will forever continue making: change takes time.

If you have seen me do a workshop, you have heard me say that I don't want you to do anything new or different in the classroom for

"ISSUES of CHANGE"

A Map/A Crutch

ISSUE: I use coloring books / Cut out pumpkins / Model art for young children

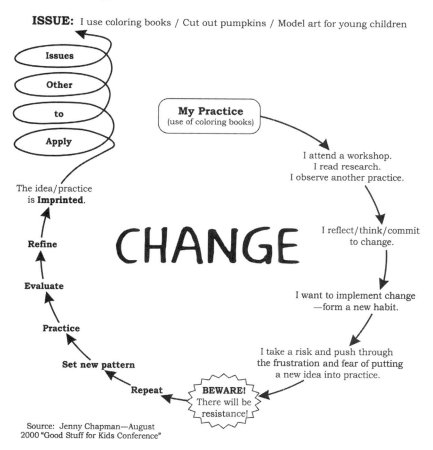

Issues

Other

to

Apply

My Practice
(use of coloring books)

I attend a workshop.
I read research.
I observe another practice.

The idea/practice
is **Imprinted**.

CHANGE

I reflect/think/commit
to change.

Refine

Evaluate

I want to implement change
—form a new habit.

Practice

I take a risk and push through
the frustration and fear of putting
a new idea into practice.

Set new pattern

Repeat

BEWARE!
There will be
resistance!

Source: Jenny Chapman—August
2000 "Good Stuff for Kids Conference"

TEN DAYS! I want you thinking (of course) about whatever you might be leaving with, but I encourage *business as usual* for the immediate ten days that follow. The only thing I want you doing differently out of the gate as you reenter your program is to really start paying attention. I want you engaged in seriously active observation. What do you see? Hear? What are you noticing? Experiencing? What conversations do you need to have with colleagues? Administration? Then after ten days, whatever is still bouncing around in your head, whatever you are still thinking about, is *your* initial baby step. (This is what I mean by TAKE TEN! Taking ten days to intentionally reflect on your conference take-aways, not instant impulsive knee-jerk reactions to them!)

If you go back to your classroom after a conference all amped up and begin changing the room around and tearing the schedule off the wall while announcing the immediate implementation of free-range napping, unlimited outdoor playtime, and the banishment of worksheets and of the UP THE STEPS AND DOWN THE SLIDE rule, as much as I commend your intention and enthusiasm, the reality is that what you are actually doing is whipping up a recipe for chaos and frustration for *everyone*! It's too fast! And that is not what I am asking you to do. What I am asking you to do is intentionally reflect on the kind of experience we say we want for the children and identify where there might be a disconnect between our words and actions.

Occasionally throughout the book I say TAKE TEN! Think of it as shorthand for making sure you don't do things too fast!

Being in this profession is a constant work in progress. We must continue adding to our theoretical arsenal and deepening our knowledge of best practice for children. To do this, we must take seriously the fact that we as individuals, with our words and our actions, have the power to positively or negatively affect the early childhood environments children are growing up in. Since we have the power to play such a huge role in their experience, it is imperative that we keep growing and learning, never losing the desire to add things to our teacher tool belts while also discarding what no longer works or is no longer relevant.

But this gets hard and sometimes we get lazy. And then we drift. As in, I used to do it more appropriately, and I know better, but I've drifted. The truth is that at some point we all drift. But there is a huge difference between drifting, realizing it, and doing something about it, and drifting, realizing it, and staying there anyway. When the choice to *stay put* (as it were) is made, it is time to move on to another job. Needing to reorient ourselves philosophically after realizing we've drifted is occasionally necessary in our profession. If and when this becomes a chore, it is time to move on. This job takes *work*. If we are after *easy*, we are going to continue to skirt the duties of what's required from us to do preschool well. As preschool people (meaning we work with children ages birth to whenever they transition to *school*), our job is to make sure that children's foundation is rock solid, so our early elementary colleagues can do their job, which is the building of the house. If I wanted to be a kindergarten teacher, a second-grade teacher, I would've been one. But like many of you reading this book, I am a *preschool* person, and that means my ethical and professional responsibility is to make sure I do preschool really really well. We *must* stay strong against pressure to start building a house where there is no foundation. Resist the push-down! Do not cave in to the pressure to do watered-down elementary school. I realize this is easy to say from behind the safety of my laptop and from the stage at a workshop, but I mean it with my heart and soul.

I might not have all the answers, but I do have a plan. A nine-point philosophical plan that will guide us as we frame of the foundation that supports the house of higher learning.

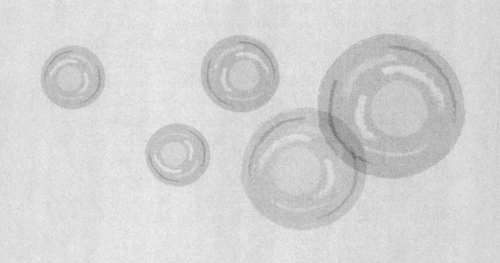

PART 4

Nine Attributes of a Child-Centered Environment

HERE ARE the nine philosophical attributes of being child centered:

1. Children are provided long periods of uninterrupted FREE TIME to explore their environment.

2. Children have lots of OUTDOOR time.

3. Children are able to explore the environment with FEW RESTRICTIONS.

4. Adults are CONTROLLING THE ENVIRONMENT, not the children.

5. Adults serve as FACILITATORS within the space.

6. Adults are able to ARTICULATE the INTENTION behind their words and actions.

7. Adults are familiar with the key contributions of historical child development THEORISTS.

8. Adults know the importance of KEEPING IT REAL.

9. Children are provided time and opportunity to CREATE, MOVE, SING, DISCUSS, OBSERVE, READ, AND PLAY (a.k.a. the seven things) each and every day.

Also remember the three additional considerations as we explore what it means to be child centered: being developmentally appropriate, nurturing strong relationships, and understanding the characteristics of play. So give the book a read, then read it again. Sounds like I'm sneaking in an assignment, doesn't it?? But listen up! While it is not my intention to sound bossy, I do need to provide a very direct cautionary statement that I hope you take very seriously. Ready?

DO NOT DO ANYTHING DIFFERENT IN YOUR PROGRAM UNTIL YOU HAVE READ THE BOOK AT LEAST ONCE.

Seriously. I really mean it. The nine attributes, being developmentally appropriate, relationships, and the importance of play are all very interconnected, so if you don't read it all the way through (at least once) before making changes to your program, your efforts might be fragmented and compartmentalized and, consequentially, not successful. We don't want that. So read it once, then read it again. The second time maybe with work colleagues, administrators, parents, or perhaps fellow students. Have discussions and conversations about your reactions to the points in the book. Be patient with yourself! Remember to TAKE TEN, then make a plan to start taking baby steps. It will be a long but *oh so very much worth it* journey. But journeys are often better with companions. So find a friend, study buddy, or coteacher and take that first step together.

Here we go.

1

Children Are Provided Long Periods of Uninterrupted Free Time to Explore Their Environment

LET'S GET RIGHT to the heart of the matter: children need more time. Time to play, explore, think, daydream, imagine, and simply be children. They deserve better than being herded like cattle from one activity to the next all day long. But let's be honest: kid time is totally different than adult time. It can often take twenty minutes to decide where to play and yet another twenty for the preplay negotiations! We are forty minutes in, and, to some adult eyes, the "play" hasn't even started yet! It can take thirty-five minutes to put on a shoe! I met a mom who told me that her three-year-old can sum up a twenty-seven-minute episode of *Paw Patrol* in seventy-two minutes. Hard-and-fast, rigid daily schedules make me antsy. Why? Because out of one side of our mouth we say we want high levels of executive function and self-regulation skills and out of the other we insist on posting daily schedules that chop a child's day up into twenty-minute time blocks. You can't have the former if you insist on the latter.

Let me elaborate. One of the current hot topics in early childhood education is the development of both executive function (EF) skills and self-regulation skills. EF skills assist children in planning, decision-making, memory, flexible shifting from one task to another, and, among other things, managing feelings as well as unwanted thoughts and emotions. Kenneth Ginsburg, lead author of the 2007 American Academy of Pediatrics report on play, tells us that free play gives children time to discover their interests and tap into their creativity and that it is a "crucial element for building resilience," which they will need to be happy, productive adults. And in their 2014 study, researcher Jane Barker and her colleagues reported that free time in children's lives predicts high levels of self-directed executive functioning.

The Center on the Developing Child at Harvard University tells us that having EF skills assists us in planning, focusing, switching gears, and juggling multiple tasks; hence executive function frequently being referred to as the air traffic control center of your brain. EF and self-regulation skills depend on three types of brain function: working memory (able to retain information over a short period of time), mental flexibility (able to sustain or shift attention in response to different demands and/or settings), and self-control (resisting impulsivity).

Here is a quick block play scenario showing these three functions in action:

Working memory: My tower fell over a minute ago. I need to remember what I did so I can adjust my building this time so it doesn't fall down again.

Mental flexibility: Hmmmmmm, I wonder how my building will be different if I construct it in the sandbox. I wonder if I can make it again but with Legos instead of wooden blocks.

Self-control: Not throwing blocks in frustration when the building falls a second time and not screaming at other kids who come too close.

Children with high EF skills are collaborative, persistent, cooperative, flexible thinkers with high levels of self-regulation—and a predictor of high EF skills is (wait for it) *long periods of free time where the children are able to direct their play and the choices they make.*

Why is this so important for us to know? Because if you scroll through *Fast Company* articles, ask any hiring manager, talk to a Fortune 500 company CEO, or even do a quick Google search of "skills employees are lacking," it won't take long to see a pattern. Sure, they can speak a couple of languages, they can code, and they are masters at search engine optimization, but they aren't collaborators, they have a hard time problem solving, and they have poor communication skills. While our culture often refers to skills like these as "soft skills," they are just as important (although ignored for so long now that I'd say they might be *more* important) as more technical ones. The Partnership for 21st Century Learning (and dare I say *common sense*) tells us that these are the skills our children will need to "be ready" for the future:

- adaptability
- agility
- attention to detail
- collaboration
- communication skills
- coping skills
- creativity
- critical thinking
- curiosity
- flexibility
- imagination
- leadership
- people skills
- problem solving
- teamwork

Do you know where and when each and every one of those skills is being crafted, nurtured, developed, practiced, and mastered? When children are playing.

Want children to be "ready"? Then they need long periods of uninterrupted free time to play. Seems pretty straightforward, right? But is it? What would you call A LONG TIME? An hour? Two? All day? Until they are done? I'd say *at least* an hour, with the ideal being that children are able to stay at a task until they choose to be done. If we claim to want high EF skills but refuse to provide the time required to nurture them, we are walking an ethical tightrope.

How would you define UNINTERRUPTED? Well if we define *interrupt* as breaking the continuity or stopping the process, then UNinterrupted means not doing those things.

And FREE TIME? When I think of *free time*, I imagine a block of time where I am able to do, think, or act without feeling obligated to do anything other than what it is I'm choosing to do at that moment. I'm not sure if anything less than an hour is anything more than a *break*. And if what I do during "free time" is chosen by someone else, it's not "free" and it is most definitely not *play*. Why not? Because of Peter Gray's first characteristic of play: that it is freely chosen and I can quit when I am done. And if what I am being told to do during "free time" is really adult-driven learning agenda in disguise, we have violated Gray's second characteristic of play as well.

But I don't want to frustrate you right off the bat. So let's change gears. Let me ask you a question. What if *right now* I told you to GO PLAY! Seriously. GO PLAY! What would you do? I'll even sweeten the deal and say GO PLAY! *and* tell you that money is no object! *Now* what would you get up and go do?

Get a massage? Go to the movies? Go shopping? Go camping? Fishing? Work on the boat? Make a cake? Clean the closets? Take a dance class? Start a game of chess?

Let's play this out. Let's pretend I told you to GO PLAY and you decided to get a full body massage: day spa, robe, slippers, champagne, the works! For kicks and giggles, I'll suspend time while you figure out how to get there. AND while you are filling out the paperwork. AND while you have that first sip. But now, you are finally in the dimly lit treatment room, there's soft soothing music, you can feel yourself relaxing, the room smells faintly of lavender, you undress, you get under the sheet (I'm still giving you a time credit here, you understand), and finally, your massage therapist comes in. TIME CREDIT, OFF! If you've never received a full body massage before, it takes about twenty minutes JUST TO DO YOUR BACK. You are finally settled in, you've shelved your anxieties about being naked in front of a stranger, you are breathing deeply and allowing yourself to receive this amazing experience, and then suddenly, BAM! I open the door, flick the lights, clap my hands, and start singing the cleanup song. YOU'D SMACK ME!

And we didn't even consider the importance of all the preliminary preplay planning and negotiating. What kind of massage? Where shall we go? Is there a Groupon? Bruno Bettelheim reminds us that the "getting ready to play" can be developmentally more important than whatever ends up getting played out. Think about it. Figuring out who gets to use the red truck or who gets the favorite shoes, all the compromising, negotiating, bartering, badgering, turn taking, and the putting of their own individual needs on pause in an effort to keep the play going are indicators of high levels of executive functioning and spot-on self-regulation skills. When we take this valuable time away from children, we deprive them of the opportunity to master the very skills we claim we want them to have.

If a pattern develops in which telling children to GO PLAY! is continually followed by way too short of a time frame to actually do it and never enough time to finish what was started, or if it becomes apparent that CLEANING UP (the product) is more important than the PLAY (the process), know what happens? You stop exploring stop investigating stop painting stop building stop negotiating stop *playing* because you reach a point of not bothering. I was told once by a group of young children, "Ms. Lisa, we used to build big block towers, but it was always time to put them away."

 BREATHE

"But we just don't have enough time!" I disagree, and I will elaborate as to why, but to do that, we need to turn our attention to the thing that is often *blamed* (although not always at *fault*) for why adults who work with children claim they don't have enough time: the schedule.

Now, do *not* get fired because you read this book. Unless you want to get fired, but that's a different conversation. What I am saying is that I do *not* want you to march back into your classroom on Monday, rip down your schedule, throw up the VICTORY "V" with your arms, and scream, "LISA MURPHY SAYS WE! DON'T! NEED! THIS!!" Because that is *not* what I am saying. Here are the things I *am* saying:

First off, let's get something clear: there is nothing inherently *wrong* with having a posted schedule (I prefer "flow to the day," but I'm not going to split hairs). Where I get itchy is when it is rigid and controlling and not the least bit flexible. Let's shelve DAP and philosophy for a minute and just be realistic: the truth of the matter is that your schedule might *say* you do circle time from 10:00 until 10:30, but the reality is that there are going to be days where circle time lasts from 10:00 to 10:05! And the VERY NEXT DAY it lasts until 11:00! You aren't going to stop the stories and songs and requests to "Read it again!" or the announcements of, "Teacher, look what I found in my pocket!" with a glib, "I'm sorry children but it appears as though we have exceeded our language and literacy allotment for the day."

And then there is another day ("What day *is* it?" asked Pooh, and Piglet squeaked, "It's today." "My favorite day," said Pooh.) when it's time to Get Ready for Circle, and as you begin gathering up all your circle time business, you look around and notice four children figuring out snaps, buttons, and ties in dress-up; five others building roads and towers in the block area; three more working at the easel (because two of them are doing a cooperative painting); four children in the sensory tub pouring, scooping, and measuring the colored rice; four more drawing pictures with the new kid, who is dictating a story; and the twins remain sprawled out on the floor figuring out the new one-hundred-piece puzzle. At that moment you stop and ask yourself a Very Important Question: *Why in the WORLD would I interrupt a room full of engaged children to come to a meeting?*

And why would you? Where did that expectation come from? Whose Kool-Aid are you drinking?

Do we feel we are "just supposed to do it"? Was it something our professor told us to do? Is there a real (or perceived) mandate? Are we worried that our director, owner, principal, a parent, licensing or someone of educational importance *might* walk in? And what? That you'd be questioned? Challenged? What specifically would you be concerned about? One of the things I am concerned about is that we are undermining the experiences our children are receiving in an effort to keep someone happy who is rarely (or never) even in the building. And to add insult to injury, many of the people we are so anxious to keep happy have no training or knowledge of early childhood education. And as much as I'd love it if they did, I don't NEED them to. What I do need is for them to trust THAT I DO and therefore can be counted on to do the job I have been hired to do in the most developmentally appropriate way possible, instead of treating me as though I am the same age as the children I work with. But for this to happen, I need to be knowledgeable, confident, and articulate. I need to trust that I have the ability to talk about what is unfolding in the classroom to anyone who walks in the door and wants to discuss what they see instead of just keeping a schedule stapled to the wall and blindly following it because that is what (I think) I am expected to do.

 ## BREATHE

I have worked in many of the individual states here in the United States. In some of them, you have to post a schedule on the wall that says at _____o'clock you are doing _____. Like, down to the minute! Not only is this an unrealistic, ridiculous expectation, it flies in the face of what we know about child development. Anyone who has ever spent an afternoon with one toddler, let alone a classroom full of them, quickly realizes that to imagine ten of them doing anything at the same time is ludicrous. Some individual states require you to list what's being offered (the flow), but they cut you some slack on needing to post an actual time, whereas some places are somewhere in between. What's my point? That before you get all in a huff about it, you need to know what is required WHEREVER YOU ARE! Canada? Australia? The United States? Europe? On a military base? The first order of business is knowing the rules and regulations that you are responsible for following. Do NOT take anyone's word for it. And I mean no disrespect to leads and supervisors, principals, or administrators! If you (as a teacher) work in a place where there *are* regulations regarding schedule requirements, YOU, yes YOU! have a responsibility to know what they are. Firsthand.

You are not allowed to just blindly accept what poopy-face down the hall told you.

This right here tells me a lot about someone's level of buy-in to their job. If going to the source and reading the regulations is too much of a hassle for you, then you have no right to be complaining about how unfair or unreasonable they might (or might not) be. End of discussion. And this might be a perfect lead-in to my favorite Carol Garhart Mooney quote: "If you don't take time to participate, then surrender your right to pontificate!" When you choose to participate (and put some legwork in), you just might discover that the time invested in reading the rules ends up giving you more time in the classroom because you might find out that the rules are not as rigid as you were told (or as you thought).

Here's another thing to consider about your schedule: many of you *inherited* your classrooms and everything that was in them. Including a schedule that, let's be honest, has been posted on that sun-faded WEL-COME! board for quite some time now. Walk over and take a good look at that schedule. Does it reflect what generally happens (for the most part) throughout the course of the day? Or do you find yourself pressured to make the children fit into it? When and where did it come to pass that we started thinking young children "learn" in short, chopped-up blocks of time? And what might happen if we **broke up** with this myth? What if we broke up with the idea of compartmentalizing their childhoods and instead considered what it might look like if we changed our minds and decided to merge some of these twenty-minute chunks together?

I'm providing for you here a typical schedule you might see in any number of classrooms. If you are in a half-day program, you might end at lunch. If you are in a religious program, add some instruction at some point; if you are working with children who have special needs, then add the one-on-one direct instruction that might be related to their IEPs somewhere in there too. If you teach kindergarten, add in any specific district- or curriculum-mandated instruction as well. But all of you, just hang in there with me—it's going to all come out in the wash as we move ahead. As much as you can, suspend your focus on details related to your specific group for the time being.

What if instead of a day looking like this:

7:00	Center Opens
	Breakfast
7:30	Potty/Wash Hands
7:45	Table Activities (puzzles, manipulatives, markers, crayons, playdough)
8:00	Science
8:20	Art
	Wash Hands
8:40	Math
9:00	Circle Time/Morning Meeting
	Potty/Wash Hands
9:30	Snack
9:45	Potty/Wash Hands
10:00	Outdoor Play
10:30	Potty/Wash Hands
10:45	Play at Centers (blocks, dress-up, easel, puppets, sensory tub)
11:15	Clean Up for Lunch
11:30	Potty/Wash Hands
11:45	Lunch
	Potty/Wash Hands
	Stories on Cots
12:30–2:30	Nap
2:30	Potty/Wash Hands
2:45	Snack
3:00	Outdoor Play
3:30	Potty/Wash Hands
	Stories/Songs
4:00	Merge with Closing Teacher in the Closing Room
4:15	Potty/Wash Hands
	Play at Centers in Closing Room
5:00	Outside Play Until Pickup
6:00	Center Closed

What if it slowly started to look like this:

. . . .

7:00   Center opens

Children are welcomed in their classroom by their teacher

Breakfast is offered to anyone hungry

Children may play/explore/investigate *any and all* areas of the classroom (including but not limited to blocks, art materials, easel, books and stories, puzzles, sensory tubs, music, writing tools, playdough and clay, dress-up, manipulatives, and various loose parts)

8:30ish   An invitation is made to join the teacher on the carpet for songs and stories

When it's over . . .

Snack

When that's over . . .

9:30ish   Outdoor play

10:30ish   Back inside to play/explore/investigate *any and all* areas of the classroom

Slow cleanup for lunch around 11:45ish

12–2:30ish   Lunch and rest

As children wake, they can read, color, or do puzzles or other quiet activities while other children are still resting

3:00ish   Snack

Then outdoor play until 4:30ish

4:30ish   Back inside to play/explore/investigate *any and all* areas of the classroom until pickup

6:00   Center closes

. . . .

Until eventually it looked like this:

- -

7:00   Center opens

Children play indoors and out (with materials including but not limited to blocks, art materials, easel, books and stories, puzzles, sensory tubs, music, writing tools, playdough and clay, dress-up, manipulatives, loose parts, obstacle courses, sand and water, and large-motor equipment that encourages climbing, throwing, running, and swinging)

Breakfast is offered in the morning to anyone who is hungry

Snack is offered throughout the day as children are hungry (yes, the first week they eat all day—but eventually they realize it's not going away and it's here if they need it, so they stop)

Lunch and rest are provided in the middle of the day, but if someone is sleepy at another time, we are advocates of free-range napping (don't you wish you had this option!)

Children continue their indoor and outdoor play

6:00   Center closes

See you tomorrow!

- -

Now before you pick up my guitar, show me the door, and tell me to not let the kumbaya hit my ass on the way out, stop for a minute. Seriously. Just stop. Let me tell you in all seriousness, having done this work for almost thirty years, it is possible to reach this point! I'll never sugarcoat it and lie to you and pretend it's easy, but I will honestly tell you that it is 100 percent *possible*. There are tons of variables that will need your attention along the way, but at the end of the day, it is possible.

I know for a fact that many of you are on a journey of really really really trying to get to this place. Some of you had the luxury of being able to jump right in, feet first! Lucky you! Some of you are as far as the current system you are in allows, good for you too! I know a few of you have quit using existing systems and started your own in your efforts to get to this place, so here's a hearty huzzah for y'all as well!

I *also* know that many of you are just starting out, feel your hands are tied, don't feel any support from coworkers or administration, or flat-out just don't think you have a choice. And at the risk of sounding teachy and preachy, I do want to lovingly remind you that there is ALWAYS a choice. You might not want to deal with the result of the choice, but you *always* have a choice, including to not make a choice. And if *not* making a choice is your choice, it might behoove you to occasionally go back and reread my favorite Carol Garhart Mooney quote from a few pages back.

So let's get back on track. I want all of you to consider the next baby step you can take on your journey. So here's your first task: I'm going to ask all of you—especially those of you who might be in the "I don't really have a choice" group—to take a minute and identify your specific reason(s) as to why you think a schedule such as the third example is *not* an option. Like, seriously, write your reason(s) right here in this box:

```
 _____

 _____

 _____

 _____

 _____
```

WHAT?! Write in a book? YES. Write in it. *But that's just . . .* wrong! Who told you that? Where did that mind-set come from? It's your book, silly. Underline it, takes notes in it, highlight it. I promise nothing bad will happen and it won't go on your permanent record! So do it. Write down your initial concerns about moving closer to schedule number three. Does the idea of a schedule that looks more like number three intrigue you? I thought so. Let's get started.

The first thing to do is to is determine when the transition will take place. How BIG of a switch is this going to be? How close are you already to a schedule that looks like number three? Can it happen midyear? Do you need to start over the summer? Would it be best to start the process of TALKING about the switch NOW and then wait until the beginning of the new school year to get it rolling? You are going to know what is best for your program!

The second thing to determine is whether this is a whole school transition or maybe just your room. This is one of the areas where family child care providers have more flexibility than the rest of us. You're the boss! In center-based programs, while ideally *all* the staff would be moving toward schedule number three, realistically, it could very well be that only Room 5 takes the plunge, and Room 6 stays stubbornly planted in schedule one. And as frustrating as this can be, unless you are in a position to *mandate* the transition of moving toward schedule three, the reality is that neither of us is the boss of Ms. Poopy Face.

 BREATHE

What's next? The next phase is getting the children acclimated to having more time and more choices. I have found the best way for this to happen is to block off *at least* two full weeks (TAKE TEN!). During this time, the children start getting used to all of the items in the room being available. Remember that *all* the areas within the space means ALL of them! Including but not limited to blocks, art materials, easels, books and stories, puzzles, sensory tubs, music, writing tools, playdough and clay, dress-up, manipulatives, and various loose parts. You may still have transitions for snack, lunch, nap, outdoor play, whatever—that's totally fine. The main focus is to get both you and the children recalibrated to the new normal of YOU NOT BEING THE BOSS OF EVERYTHING.

The children are going to test this. Depending on how controlling you may have been, this could be a smooth transition or it might get a little rough. Be patient. There are two goals during this initial phase: the first goal is to have the children relax into the new normal of being able to have long periods of free time to explore and start directing their own playful learning within the space while you move into the role of facilitator. Everyone is, in essence, going through a CONTROL detox.

The second goal of this initial phase is that you (the adult) start practicing how to link all the playful learning that is occurring to the four domains within DAP. Like for real. Like homework. What are you observing? What developmental domains can you link your observations to? Cognitive? Language and literacy? Social and emotional? Physical? All of them? Start keeping track in whatever method or manner works for you so you become comfortable and skilled at being able to articulate how the playful learning you observe can be linked to developmental goals, which in turn can be linked to curricular ones.

Then, after the children (and you!) get comfortable within this new pattern, you can do any kind of one-on-one, small-group pullout, direct instruction that may be required without having to be overly preoccupied with the other children. I'm not implying that you should be doing this; I just know that many of you reading have this kind of expectation placed on you. And for those of you who don't have this kind of program expectation, the children recalibrating to this new normal is good for you as well. Why? Because all those areas or centers (whatever your language had been) which may have previously been seen as a "special treat" have now become just what we do here. Playful exploration within the other areas of the classroom is now the new normal. And the result of this is beautiful. You are able to give the children in front of you your undivided attention—for some kind of small-group direct instruction, this could be simply assisting children as they navigate daily interactions with their peers, reading a book to a few interested kids, helping one of them learn to tie shoes, facilitating turn-taking, or whatnot—and because the other areas of the room are no longer "special treats," the materials and children in them no longer need to be micromanaged. Now add to this the fact that you are strengthening your ability to link all of what's happening to the four domains of DAP for anyone who walks in and questions why those kids are *playing* while these kids are *learning*, and you have the planted the seeds of a success-ful transition toward schedule number three.

What about specific or unique environments? Well here are a few things about your program I don't get overly focused on: the name on your door; profit or nonprofit; private or public; free lunch or organic and catered; after-school care, full day, half day; forest school or nature-based; what overarching philosophy or classical method you subscribe to, whether that be Montessori, Reggio, Waldorf; religious or not; the demographics of the children and families; children with special needs, who are medically fragile, or who are on the spectrum; or children who are gifted or otherwise. Why not? Because if you are focused on the children, focused on your relationships with them and their families, and 100 percent committed to being a child-centered professional who supports playful learning, you will figure out ways to responsibly meet the specific-to-your-population-nonnegotiable goals without compro-mising DAP.

You CAN meet your obligations and still be developmentally appro-priate. Again, it's not easy, but it is *possible*, which is why I get so sad when folks tell me they feel forced to choose between one or the other. I realize that not everyone reading this has a room full of develop-mentally typical children. Some of you are working with children who require very specific interactions and interventions, and I am not in any position (either via training or experience) to tell any of you what that should look like or how it's to be done. What I am in a position to do is lovingly remind everyone reading this book that *all* children everywhere have the right to a developmentally appropriate, playful childhood, whether they have an IEP or not.

 BREATHE

Reality check: Occasionally you might find yourself in a situation where there is an expectation (or six) that is, as we say, noncompromisable. What do you do in these situations? QUIT AND START YOUR OWN PROGRAM! Ha! Kidding not kidding! But seriously, if you aren't quite yet ready to take that big leap, until you are, I offer for your consideration the only phrase (to date) that I have coined: you will need to be as *developmentally inappropriately appropriate as possible*. It's like a tongue twister! Put it in your tool belt for when you need it. Example: Let's say that a nonnegotiable expectation in Teacher Mark's pre-K room is that he is expected to do daily small-group direct instruction with the provided Kute Korporate Kiddie Kurriculum (I'm suspending my judgment on this expectation in an effort to keep the example going), but both he and the children have transitioned to a schedule more like number three, where the children are used to playing/exploring/investigating *any and all* areas of the classroom. He is probably going to find this non-compromisable curriculum expectation easier to swallow because he knows that at all other times of the day, the children are engaged in playful learning AND if someone walked in and challenged it, he is confident that he has the tools in his tool belt (read: can link it all back to DAP) to translate it for the person who doesn't see it. In this situation he is being as *developmentally inappropriately appropriate as possible*.

Here's a success story for you: Recently I had a conference call with two kindergarten teachers and their principal, and we were talking about how to approach this kind of transition in their classrooms. I asked if, for whatever reason, the school district mandates direct instruction in math with Curriculum A and language and literacy with Curriculum B, what would happen if AT ALL THE OTHER TIMES OF THE DAY the children were playing/exploring/investigating any and all areas of the classroom? Then we spent a considerable amount of time talking about what it might look like! I walked them through the TAKE TEN schedule transition, suggesting that the first two weeks of school would be set aside for the children to play and explore the room and the materials in it, while the teachers could observe interactions and which materials were (or were not) being used, as well as generally facilitate as the children calibrate to this being the norm. Only after providing the time necessary for children to acclimate to the room, the materials, and the expectations would the teachers start the district-mandated instruction (they called them "pullouts"). So while the teacher is at the table with a small group, the rest of the students can be playing in the other areas of the room. Nothing was a special treat, nothing was saved for "when the work was done"—it was all always available. I was thrilled when at the end of the phone call the principal said he was willing to support the entire kindergarten teaching team as they implemented this new plan for the upcoming school year! How exciting to hear a principal acknowledge that the teachers had been correct when they said children are learning all day long, not just when they are sitting at a desk or a table!

Back when I did family child care, newly enrolled families would sometimes ask, "What is your schedule?" and I'd say, "You can drop them off after six a.m. and need to pick them up by six p.m.!" And while many were receptive to this, others wanted to know, "But when do you do math? Science? Art? Reading?" Guess what, guys? If you are grounded in DAP and research-based best practices, the honest (and accurate) answer is what? That's right! *All. Day. Long.*

Let's unpack this a little. Flip back a few pages and look at that first schedule. The chopped-up time block one. Really look at it. When we have a posted schedule that compartmentalizes the various learning or curriculum areas, it sends a very strong visual message that math, for example, is only happening at 8:40 a.m., when in fact, *if we are doing it right*, when are we "doing" math? That's right! A gold star for you! ALL. DAY. LONG.

Stay with me now. So if we say that we do math, and *then* science, and *then* reading, and *then* (later) we play, this sends an incorrect message that the learning needs to stop for the play to happen AND that there's no play or playfulness within the learning: this, kids, is what we call the *false dichotomy* of learning versus play. That one has to stop for the other to occur, and this is simply not true.

Jump back again and take another peek at schedule number three, and let's continue thinking about what needs to happen for us to start moving in that direction. I've already given you an overarching and general plan of attack, but let's get a little more specific. Once you decide on your TAKE TEN start date, don't make a grand announcement. Don't send a note home saying that you are going to revamp the schedule. You'll get calls and emails from now 'til the cows come home. Just start doing it. I'd argue that you are better served leaving your schedule posted *as is* for a little bit of time while you start changing your practice in real time. Why? Well, mostly because you are going to need practice dealing with people who don't get it! Let's act this one out:

* *

A PERSON WHO DOESN'T GET IT (PWDGI) walks into the classroom of a TEACHER WHO SUPPORTS PLAYFUL LEARNING (TWSPL). The PWDGI glances at the posted schedule, then around the room, and looks confused. Before speaking, they loudly clear their throat to get TWSPL's attention, and they point to the schedule and begin talking.

PWDGI: Says here you should be _____ right now, and all I see is a bunch of kids playing!

TWSPL: You're noticing that the schedule says that at ten o'clock we _____. And you are concerned because you don't see any _____ happening.

PWDGI: Well, yes! Yes I am!

TWSPL: Do you mind telling me, specifically, what you *do* see happening?

PWDGI: Well those kids are just stacking up blocks, and those kids are just messing around with playdough, and the kids at the table just got a bunch of buttons strewn all over. Those two are just lying around on their bellies on the carpet flipping pages of a book, and the kids over there are putting on a bunch of old clothes, and . . .

* *

Why did I stop there? Because your secret weapon at this point is knowing *without a doubt* that YOU have the ability to link a developmental benefit to each and every one of the PWDGI's observations. You might not actually need to, but you need to know you *could* if the situation called for it. You must continue making sure that you are getting really really good at being able to identify what is happening in the room when the children are (how did I say it?) playing/exploring/investigating *any and all* areas of the classroom.

How *does* playdough link to cognitive development? Language and literacy? Social-emotional development? Physical development?

What about sorting a bunch of buttons? Stacking blocks? Playing dress-up?

We will do this linking in depth later in the book, but I want you to start thinking about it now.

If I have set up the space in a developmentally appropriate fashion, it really shouldn't matter where the children choose to play or how long they stay there. Why don't we let them self-select where they'd like to play? Why do they always have to be in a large group? Moving yourself and the children like a herd of cattle through the daily schedule is the second thing I'd like you to **break up** with. Everyone to math! Everyone to art! Everyone to circle! Mooooo! How about instead of thinking we all have to move to the *same place* at the *same time* in an effort to stay on schedule, we started strengthening our ability to identify and articulate what is happening in the block area, the dress-up area, the sensory tub, or the art easel and linking it back to DAP for folks who don't see it on their own? I know I have repeated this in various ways here, there, and everywhere, but I really do think being confident in our ability to link play to the four developmental domains of DAP is our secret weapon!

When a PWDGI walks in and asks, "What are they doing?" We often *hear*, "You shouldn't be doing that!" or "That's not allowed!" But that is *not* what was said at all; it's what we *heard*. And if that's what you think you're constantly hearing, you will start convincing yourself that blocks, ooblick, playdough (whatever) aren't *allowed*, when really we overreacted to what we *heard* instead of responding to what was *said*. So instead of having a knee-jerk reaction and thinking that so-and-so said the kids can't play with blocks anymore, start translating what's happening in the block area for the folks who don't see it on their own.

The more time we spend considering the literal and philosophical importance of *time*, the easier it is to consider the other elements of being a child-centered teacher. It all takes time! Shoot, it can take some honest to goodness *time* for you to even start thinking it's important. We begin to find lots of *time* in the schedule when we start to see (and be able to articulate) the value of what *is* happening instead of thinking that what is happening needs to stop for us to do the "important stuff."

What's happening *is* the important stuff. But you need to take the *time* to make sure you believe that.

If all this sounds like too much work, or seems too hard, or you just don't think you have the time, it may be time for you to go. Or take a break. I really don't want to sound like I'm giving you an ultimatum or a thousand extra assignments, but I want to make it really clear that the *time* invested in some of these after-hour things is often a one-time investment that pays you back dividends! It is *time* invested in your own professional growth and development *and* into the quality of your program. As I say in my workshops, I am well aware of the fact that these are not the fun, sexy parts (I said *sexy parts*!) of our industry! But they must be done IF, and I say IF, we are ready to put our money where our mouth is and start taking responsibility for some of the inconsistent practices in our profession. If you claim to be child centered and a supporter of playful learning but have no intention of ever cracking open your state or provincial licensing regulations, you never plan on making a quick bullet-point list of how all of your learning centers link back to the developmental domains within DAP, you have absolutely no business in this profession.

This is not a call to arms to eliminate daily schedules—it is a challenge to rethink them. The ultimate goal is to provide long periods of uninterrupted free time. The realistic first baby step may be finding A Little More Time. Maybe you "let" the children have ten extra minutes before flicking the lights and singing the cleanup song. Maybe you mush together two of the things on the schedule (today it's time for math AND science), thus providing a little more time to explore these topics, and (bonus!) eliminating at least two unnecessary transitions! When this happens, you will notice changes, I promise. The room doesn't feel as crazy, you are not as stressed, and behavior problems decrease.

Our exploration of time is both literal and philosophical. From the literal perspective, it's what we just did in the previous pages, identifying how we can provide long periods of uninterrupted free time for children to experience developmentally appropriate playful learning. Philosophically, well, that's where we are headed next.

When the room is in that flow state of the children exploring, talking, playing, working, we may find we have more time to start really seeing the children. When this happens, we deepen our relationships with them, thus increasing the opportunity for more meaningful conversations. On the other hand, when we feel pressed for time, we can fall into the cycle of asking fake questions instead of real ones. A fake question is when it sounds like the child has a choice in the matter but really they don't. Here are my two favorite fake questions:

You guys ready to go back inside?

You guys ready for bed?

The way I posed these questions implied that the children had a choice. But in reality, they didn't, so the children, thinking they're being given a choice, holler out a resounding "NO!" to which I holler back, "Line up!" or "Get on your nap mat!" Why did I imply that there was a choice if there really wasn't one? If it's time to go in, say, "It's time to go in!" Don't ask! This is the third thing I am going to challenge you to **break up** with: asking fake questions. Ever ask a young child, "Can Ms. Lisa sit down next to you?" and have them respond with a flat-out no? You'll quit cold turkey after that. I did.

If you work with younger children, take the time to be mindful of how often you use the phrase "Can you [fill in the blank]?" If you are asking children all day things like, "Can you put your coat on?" "Can you put this over on the shelf?" "Can you wash your hands?" "Can you clean your room?" "Can you fold the sheet?" They might tell you YES, but then not DO it! Then you call me in frustration saying "They don't follow directions!" and after I tell you to BREATHE I will lovingly tell you that *you were not giving any!* We forget that toddlers and younger preschoolers do not "hear" the polite request hidden in the question the way older children and adults do. To younger children, it appears as though we are

> **Things to Break Up with Review List**
>
> twenty-minute time blocks
>
> moving like a herd
>
> asking fake questions

gathering information, not asking them to do something. I'd venture a guess that each and every one of you reading has called an adult friend on the phone and when their child answered, you asked, "Is your mama there?" and after they answered, "Yes!" they promptly hung up on you. It's the exact same thing—to their ears you are gathering information, and they don't get the subtext yet! Please remember that we get in the habit of asking fake questions NOT because we are bad people who don't care about conversations, but because we are rushed, pressed for time, and not thinking about what is coming out of our mouths. I want you to take the *time* to start doing just that.

Early in my career I started saying (of my classroom), "This is a child's place and we move at a child's pace." I posted it over the doorway of one of the rooms I worked in. I started sharing it at conferences too. People always bent over their notebooks after I said it, so I started to think that maybe they were writing it down. I wondered if it still resonated with them on Monday. It later came to pass that a child care center in Indiana painted it as a mural in the entry of their school. I was invited to see it after it was completed and was both honored and embarrassed at the same time that someone would want to put something I said on a wall—the wall everyone looked at every day as they walked into the school. She said, "But Lisa, that's exactly why we did it."

I later worked with a teacher who painted her own sign for her room. It said, "There is nothing more important than what we are doing right now."

Read that again.

"There is nothing more important than what we are doing right now."

Then ask yourself if you believe it. Of course you will say that you do. Now ask yourself if a nonbiased outside observer would believe you if they spied on your classroom for a few hours. Calm down, calm down, I'm not throwing anyone under the bus, nor am I being judgmental. I am encouraging you to take the time to consider some of the disconnects between what we say we believe in and what we actually do.

No one will ever say they disagree with her amazing quote. But through the course of a stressful, rainy Monday morning with a new kid showing up that the director forgot to tell you about, McKenzie secretly hiding in the dress-up area trying to get the gold high-heels on before you are able to notice, Jamal losing his binkie, and Emma ("Sorry!") pooping in the car just as the parents pulled in (yeah right), we often forget. We are so overly focused on making sure we round everyone up for Morning Meeting juuuuust in case the district supervisor comes in because she said she might stop in on Monday, that we honestly forget that right now, Morning Meeting doesn't mean a hill o' beans to ANYONE in the room, not to you, not to the children, and especially not to the new kid and his mama who just want to know where to put all his *things*.

 BREATHE

Watch now as I show you how having long periods of uninterrupted free time and living the quote (instead of just having it on a poster) becomes much easier when the logistical elements we just discussed are in place. The stressful morning scenario I just shared would play out entirely differently in a classroom with a teacher-directed schedule and twenty-minute time blocks (schedule number one) and an open-ended one (schedule number three).

In the first room, the children are accustomed to *not* being allowed to "do anything" until the teacher says it's time. So now you have a room full of kids who aren't being given direction, running around, assuming they aren't allowed to X, Y, or Z yet. You are trying to welcome Taylor, the new student, but are totally distracted by the children who are running through the room. The new parent is frantic, you can smell the poopy diaper, you are preoccupied with worrying that the district supervisor will actually walk in, and where *is* that gosh-darn binkie??!!

Congratulations, you are now in full-blown panic, fight-or-flight, toxic stress, triage-the-crisis mode. The kids pick up on this, they follow your lead, they get louder, the new parent leaves in tears, McKenzie tells you that Emma stinks, you take a deep breath, put on your No-Everything-Is-Just-Fine smile, and get on with the day.

Now imagine the same scenario except that in this classroom, the children know that when they come in, they can simply START PLAYING.

Same exact situation with a couple of important exceptions: first, you have become very confident in your ability to link what's happening to the developmental domains within DAP, so it doesn't matter who shows up this morning wanting to know "What's going on here?" because your confidence in this department has skyrocketed! Second, children are able to come in and get busy in a room that is already set up in anticipation of their arrival! Kids aren't running around waiting to be told that a center is open, because they are *all* always open. They can come in and choose where they want to be. Still feeling a little sleepy and want some quiet? Books and pillows are over there for you. Ready to build and be more active? Blocks and trucks are ready and waiting! Feeling creative? There's paper at the easel and the paint cups are already filled! McKenzie isn't "getting away with anything" because the dress-up area is always open and available for her and anyone else for that matter. The room enters that flow state, you can feel that buzz, that hum of engaged children at play with materials that are relevant and meaningful to them.

Reminder: this is the goal of that initial TAKE TEN, getting to the point of recalibrating so this flow state is the new normal.

Emma gets her diaper changed while you are talking and welcoming Taylor and his mama. You are able to do this because the changing table faces the rest of the room, and you have everyone in your line of sight. The room is filled with choices that the children have *every day*, they know the drill. *You* might be a little thrown off with the addition of an unexpected new student, but because the children have this routine *every day*, they can go about the business of playing while you do what needs to happen to get Taylor somewhat settled in the room. In this classroom, unlike the other, YOU are the only one being thrown a curveball. In the other classroom it was you AND the students, a disastrous combination! And because you are an adult, you can handle it. Sure, you might be a little embarrassed that you didn't know Taylor was starting today, but because you weren't worried about needing to micromanage the other kids, you were still able to pay good attention to Taylor and his mama. Relationship status? OFF TO A GOOD START! And so what if breakfast is a little late? Nothing was more important than greeting Taylor and his mama on their first day. Breakfast can wait.

The title of my keynote address is "What If Today Was Their Only Day?" This plays into our philosophical exploration of the importance of time as well. What if, for whatever reason, today ended up being Taylor's only experience in an early childhood environment? Run that scenario through BOTH of those classroom examples. What might his memory of each place be? What about his mama's? How do our actions and words influence these memories on a daily basis?

I used to own a child care center in upstate New York. The playground was divided in half with one side for the infants and toddlers and the other for the preschoolers. Both sides had their own huge in-ground sandbox, but the one on the preschoolers' side was massive! And while I'm sure there were daily grumblings as the teachers fumbled with the tarp and the cinderblocks used as weights, they did what needed to be done because they knew it was an awesome sandbox! ANYWAY, one summer night it poured massive rain! Buckets of it! Like cats and dogs! Needless to say, the next morning the sandbox was flooded. All the rain had fallen on top of the tarp and the sandbox now looked like an in-ground pool with a blue bottom. "Great," I sarcastically thought, "now licensing is gonna show up and cite me for having a pool!"

What transpired later that morning was one of those magical things you couldn't plan if you tried. The preschool classes were outside and, of course, they wanted to use the sandbox. I watched how the teachers responded. None of them said it was *closed*. None of them used their adult strength to just heave-ho the waterlogged tarp off the sandbox. All the lead teacher said was, "Looks like it's covered in water." And that's all it took for the kids to disband in an enthusiastic effort to find cups, buckets, containers, anything that would assist. A few kids grabbed a box of the small paper cups we had in the yard for drinking water, I didn't stop them.

Want to know what determination, focus, and cooperation looks like? Twenty preschoolers bailing out a one-hundred-square-foot sand-box with Dixie cups. Want to see stick-with-it-ness? The same children NOT STOPPING until that sucker was dry. Want to see ingenuity and problem solving? When a few ran and brought the long pieces of gut-ter so the water would go farther from the sandbox and not just pool up around the edges. Want to know what real STEM looks like? When another crew determined that to get rid of the puddles that *had* accumulated around the edges they should dig irrigation trenches so the water moved down the hill, when a couple more started digging canals to try to get the water to move all the way down the hill to the asphalt, and when a kid stood up from his work and announced that the trench he dug was one hundred miles long!

Two hours later . . .

 POP QUIZ!

Identify three ways this scenario was encouraging development in the four developmental domains within DAP!

Cognitive development:

1. _____

2. _____

3. _____

Social-emotional development:

1. _____

2. _____

3. _____

Language and literacy development:

1. _____

2. _____

3. _____

Physical development:

1. _____

2. _____

3. _____

Were these teachers *teaching*? Were these children *learning*? Were these children *playing*? YES! YES! And YES! What could possibly have been more important than what they were doing right in that moment?

Quotes sometimes sink to sound-bite status and lose their oomph and credibility, but I still offer you the three I've shared so far as inspiration as you examine the deeper reasons why we need to provide children with enough time.

This is a child's place and we move at a child's pace.

What could possibly be more important than what we are doing right now?

What if today was their only day?

If we are always looking at what is coming next, we miss out on what is unfolding right in front of us. If we are always in a hurry to clean it up, we shortchange the children of the time they need to fully engross themselves in play. When children aren't hurried or interrupted, they get long periods of uninterrupted free time, which allows for deep discoveries, meaningful conversations, playful learning, and, dare I say, the acquisition and development of *essential* lifelong skills such as adaptability, agility, collaboration, flexibility, negotiation, communication, imagination, and problem solving.

2

Children Have Lots of Outdoor Time

LET'S CUT RIGHT to the chase with one of my favorite questions to ask teachers and providers: What if you stayed outside with your kids ALL DAY? The answers I've received have ranged from downright negative—"We can't do it! No way!"—to pessimistic—"They'll get sunburned!" "Not enough shade!" "The kids would get bored!"—to a level of optimism that borders on dreamy! Wonderfully descriptive fantasies of children in bare feet, climbing trees, stacking rocks, digging in sand and dirt, making mud pies, dragging logs to a stream in an effort to cross over to the other side, engaging in detailed negotiations in an effort to build a fort, sketching flowers, looking at bugs, catching sight of a deer or other animal, watching the clouds, fishing, building a campfire and maybe eating and napping around it too. Those are strong images that lift our souls and give us a moment of hope before heading back to our boring, institutionalized, risk-free, plastic playgrounds sitting atop an asphalt jungle.

> At a time when teachers are focusing their attention on formal learning confined to the classroom, Dr. Katherine Read Baker re-affirms the child's need and right to learn from the wider world outside.

Guess when this was written. (I wish that we could have one of those lift the flap things to see the answer). Guess!

1966.

It's from the introduction to Katherine Read Baker's book *Let's Play Outdoors*, published by NAEYC. Shoot, I wasn't even born in 1966, which means many of you weren't born, which means, shut up! Some of your *parents* weren't even born! We have been talking about the importance of playing outside for SO LONG that the topic itself is old enough to consider retirement! Do the math. For over fifty years we have been advocating for outdoor play. Not just recess and gym class, but long periods of free play that takes place outside. In nature. Preferably without a lot of adults hovering around.

So why do children need to have outdoor play? Because it's good for them, that's why. Know what has happened in the last half-century as free play without a lot of adult control has decreased? Childhood mental disorders, especially emotional ones such as depression and anxiety, have skyrocketed. Resilience is down, obesity is up. Vitamin D levels are down, diabetes is up. There is ample research to support that this is not a coincidence. The irony here is that we keep children inside to keep them safe, yet by doing so we are setting them up for high blood pressure, increased likelihood of nearsightedness, and, in the words of Peter Gray, mental breakdowns.

Our inconsistency knows no bounds. I am sitting here surrounded by at least ten articles and research reports outlining the emotional and medical benefits of children playing outside, yet 40 percent of the elementary schools in the United States still don't even have recess. Out of one side of our mouth we say we want kids learning, but for that to happen, they need to be moving around, and we've been taking that away from them for far too long.

Where did you play when you were little? What did you do there? What was the riskiest thing you did there? (Does your mother know?) What is the riskiest thing your students are "allowed" to do? Who did you play with? Where were the adults? How long did you get to stay out there? Did you ever play in the rain? The snow? The sun? Ever been barefoot outdoors? How about your students? Could you go back to where you played today?

What would have to happen for our children's answers to "What did you do at school today?" start to sound like the ones you just gave me?

In many instances the outdoor experiences our children are having are greatly altered from the ones we had. They are way more planned, scheduled, (supposedly) safe, and organized than the ones many of us experienced. And there are waaaaaay more adults around nowadays. I am the oldest of five kids, our mom would open up the sliding-glass door and tell us to get out and go play! We went back when we got hungry. That's it. We figured it out. We never got *bored*. Occasionally a kid *thought* he was bored so he went back home and told as much to his mom. After spending the rest of the afternoon dusting and vacuuming, he wised up, realized his mistake, and, not surprisingly, *never ever* got bored *ever* again.

I am thankful for memories of being told to come home when the streetlights came on, drinking from a hose, climbing trees, being gone for hours riding bikes with random kids from the neighborhood, spontaneous games of dodgeball and kickball in the vacant lot at the end of the block, but don't get me wrong, I am not romantically pining for the old days. Instead of *wishing* that today's children got what I did, I spend my time creating environments that offer as many of these opportunities as possible, even though it can be challenging and sometimes frustrating! Yes, we have ratios and we have to share the space with fourteen other programs, and yes, there are rules and regulations, and yes, sometimes the weather is rotten, and I swear if that shed gets broken into one! more! time! I get it! It can occasionally be a challenge to make time for long periods of daily outdoor play, but it's worth it. And based on all the research supporting the benefits of it, to not provide it borders on negligence.

But now we are faced with a conundrum: We have been reducing recess and outdoor play for so long now that some of the younger (newest?) members of our profession might not have received the same kind of open-ended outdoor play experiences that the rest of us did. And that is something worth noting. Why? Because if we know children need lots of outdoor play but the adults hanging out with them never spent much time outside, how will the crop of new early childhood professionals come to believe that it's actually important? Just because I TELL YOU it is important doesn't mean you'll believe me. Our profession is currently facing what I call "the pipeline problem," which is my shorthand way of acknowledging that the early childhood experience many of our newcomers got is very different from the one they should've received. And out of this comes the question: *How do you give back what you did not get?*

The honest answer is that you can't. Not unless you change your mind. At the risk of reducing a legitimate concern to a sound bite, *you are going to teach the way you were taught*, so unless you actually received a somewhat developmentally appropriate educational experience, you are going to need to do some work. Some hard work. Especially if you find yourself filtering everything through a very human response of, "But *I* only got twenty minutes outside and I turned out OK!" The truth is that you should've received more. Why? Because children need to be playing outside! Why?

Being outside is the only place where you are going to experience nature and the natural world. Sure, we can spend all day Google searching images of the ocean and beaches and watching YouTube videos of folks on a hike through the forest, but those images will never be able to replace the sensory experience of the real thing. In his book *Last Child in the Woods: Saving Our Children from Nature-Deficit Disorder*, author Richard Louv reminds us that the benefits of playing outside go far beyond cognitive development and better health: the outdoors is also where children gain a sense of wonder and intrigue with the natural world. You don't learn about what's OUT there by staying IN here. Being outside is how we learn to value and appreciate the natural world and the things in it: trees, lakes, oceans, birds, mountains, parks. I know I am being extreme, but it needs to be said: Do we really think children are going to evolve into environmental stewards who care about climate change or saving the polar bears when they have never even been to the woods, played in the mud, or spent time watching squirrels chase each other up and down a tree in the backyard? If these connections haven't been made, serious environmental concerns can become too overwhelming and may cause potential activists to shut down their efforts.

You have to value something before you appreciate a call to arms to save it, and it's difficult to value something if you have never forged an emotional connection with it. And creating emotional connections takes time. Children and adults alike might need to renew their interest in and connection to the outdoor world. Some children forge emotional connections with the outdoor environment by appearing very quiet in it, looking at bugs, lying in the grass and looking up at the clouds, collecting some things in their pockets and poking other things with sticks. Others have a more kinesthetic, full-body relationship with the yard. There is literally more room for some children when they are outside. The outdoor space might be the only place where no one is harping on them to BE QUIET and SIT STILL and PUT ON YOUR SHOES! In her book *The Great Outdoors: Restoring Children's Right to Play Outside*, author Mary Rivkin identifies many reasons why children need to be playing outside. One of them is that there is freedom outside. Freedom to run, jump, climb, yell, roll, throw, spin, chase . . . freedom to engage in activities and behaviors that might not be allowed anyplace else. Freedom to try something new, to push personal physical boundaries. But pushing personal physical boundaries often begins to look like risky play, and that makes plenty of adults worried. More on this in a few pages! (Tease!)

Ideally, early childhood environments would be set up, designed, and staffed in such a way that children could be inside or outside as they pleased. The resistance here is that our culture continues to think that outside time is wasted time, time taken away from *learning*, yet the research shows the complete opposite. Ask any kindergarten teacher about grasping abilities nowadays. Kids can't hold pencils. Why not? Because the fine-motor skills required to hold a pencil are lacking. And why is that? Because when outdoor play and recess are limited, large-motor muscles that support the development of the fine-motor ones are not able to get strong. Children often appear to not pay attention, yet studies have shown that activities in outdoor green spaces (versus indoor settings) decrease ADHD symptoms, but we still don't let them go outside and continue to build "playgrounds" on barren, boring surfaces. We get concerned when children appear fidgety. But "fidgety" is really just lack of core strength and balance in disguise. Know how to increase core strength and develop balance? Running around and playing outdoors for long periods of time. In the wise words of Angela Hanscom, author of *Balanced and Barefoot*, "For children to learn, they need to pay attention, in order to pay attention, we need to let them move."

Since playing outside is the best place for a child to be working on large-muscle motor development, you'd think at this point we'd be beyond debating and arguing the importance of outdoor play. Physical development has its own domain within DAP! I know many of you are bending over backward to make sure children get enough time to play outside, but there are still too many places where all they get are two sessions of twenty, maybe thirty, minutes of daily outdoor play, as we stand around, slurping our sodas, scratching our heads and wondering why we have an obesity crisis. There are already enough barriers to outdoor play, and with all the evidence showing us how critical it is for children to be playing outside, we need to make sure we aren't adding to the list. What holds us back from providing more time outside? What are we worried about? Mud, sand, water, sun, snow, bugs, wind, snails, snakes, dirt, grass, parental or administrative pressures? It is imperative that we identify actual or perceived barriers and then PUSH THROUGH THEM!

For example, you don't get sick from playing outside in the cold. So if you've been clinging to that old myth, you need to know IT DONE BEEN BUSTED! Being outside in the cold (yet fresh) air doesn't make you sick; being cooped up in an overheated classroom which is already filled with viruses and bacteria and NO fresh air, does. There are tons of resources online that provide quick, concise summaries of the benefits of outdoor winter play—keep copies on hand to share if this comes up as a barrier to outdoor play.

Concerns about clothing can be another common barrier. Ask families to provide a couple sets of extra clothes at the time of enrollment (thrift stores are amazing!) AND be responsible and inform potential clients that children play outside daily. If you go outside every single day regardless of weather, prospective families need to know this so they can make an informed choice at the time of enrollment. And if you are an administrator, you need to tell this to potential employees as well, for the same reason. You need to remove the barrier, or shall I say, the *excuse* of clothing being why you are limiting outdoor play. DO NOT modify what you tell staff or clients based on what you think they want to hear! It's rude, it's inconsistent, and it undermines not only the credibility of your program but the profession as a whole.

Now, about the extra clothes, I realize not every family is in a position to do this. So stack the deck in your favor! You can find lots of child-size clothing at yard sales! Have some "borrow clothes" and "borrow shoes" so everyone can participate without fear of punishment for dirty stuff, or frustration with having to do laundry every night! In tandem with providing extras, do your due diligence and let parents know that their children aren't going home muddy because staff wasn't paying attention! We sometimes forget that Mom and Dad didn't see the process of it all—they may just see the end result. No one said, "Put all this paint on your body!" But when he instigated it on his own, no one got all bent out of shape. Children are washable, and so are their clothes. It's not the rain that makes us crazy, it's that no one has boots or umbrellas. It's not the snow *per se*, it's the missing glove and the boots that are, seemingly overnight, now two sizes too small.

If there is a perceived licensing (or some kind of regulatory body) barrier to outdoor play, pull out those rules and regulations and read them! One time at a workshop we discovered that there was a commonly held belief among the teachers in the audience that they were not allowed to go outside if it was colder than twenty degrees Fahrenheit. But when the regulations were actually consulted, it was discovered that the phrasing was that you *had* to go out if it was twenty or above. There was no language regarding a temperature threshold of when they couldn't go out. Somewhere along the way this regulation had been either misunderstood or misinterpreted, thus leading to a commonly held (mis)belief that they couldn't go outside if it was colder than twenty degrees. Yet in actuality, there was no such language in the regulations at all.

Be proactive! If you know you get hot when it's overly warm, dress accordingly, get a hat, and have your water bottle and sunglasses ready to go. When it gets chilly, be mindful of "I'm cold, we're going in!" syndrome! If you're cold, get a jacket.

There was a teacher who used to work for me a long time ago who had everyone convinced that during the winter you had to call the "weather line" to see if you were allowed to take the children outside. (I know, right?!) Come to find out, she was calling her *mother*. There was no weather line. She just didn't want to be bothered with the hassle of getting fifteen three-year-olds ready to go outside in the winter, and you know what?! I don't blame her! It takes forever and can be as frustrating as an attempt at herding cats, but guess what??? That's our job! I know we can zip coats faster, tie boots quicker, and get little fingers shoved into gloves quick-time, double-time, go! Go! Go! I also know that when we let children do it themselves (which we know we should, because *how else are they going to learn how to do it?),* we know we should be patient, yet we find ourselves mentally pulling our hair out as they tumble all over each other like baby pandas because all that gear weighs more than they do! We cry on the inside as we watch the minutes *tick-tock-tick-tock* turn into what feels like hours as our thirty minutes of outdoor play now *tick-tock-tick-tock* turns into ten because *tick-tock-tick-tock* it takes twenty to get them dressed!

What's the rush? What's the hurry? That it is going to take too long to get ready and we are going to miss our turn in the yard? What really is at the *core* of this scenario that might be stressing us out? That we need some assistance? That there are too many kids in the room? Perceived or real pressure to be staying on schedule? A feeling that we need to hurry up and get OUT so we can come back IN and get back to work? All of these things become barriers to more time outside. Not all of the barriers are external. Sure, it might be easier to pass the buck and blame licensing regulations or something like that, but an important piece of the puzzle is becoming comfortable with being honest with ourselves and reflecting on what we bring to the table without embarrassment or self-shaming. If there is a little secret hidden place within your soul that kinda thinks that playing outside *is* a little bit of a waste of time, you need to admit it, shake it off, and let it go! Let's face it, many of you are under huge amounts of pressure to be doing *things* with children. And many of these *things* that someone says you should be doing are inside things. Therefore, it is entirely possible that at some point you are going to come to the realization that you, (we, us, them, me) have drifted away from best practice. Drifted far. Possibly far enough to where even the most play-based of us wakes up one morning in a panic of realization that we started believing what we've been told, even though we knew better. How do we come back to center? If you find that you—for whatever reason—*have* started to lose sight of why outdoor play is important, don't beat yourself up and overthink it! Instead, let yourself go back and consider the four developmental domains within DAP. What are they? Cognitive, language and literacy, social-emotional, and what? Boom! There it is! Physical.

Physical development has its own domain. This means that large-(gross) motor and small- (fine) motor skill development is just as important as the other stuff. Ignoring this in the name of readiness is being unethical and inappropriate. Remind yourself how children grow: from the neck down and the trunk out! What does this mean? It means that while there are elements of small- and large-motor development that are happening concurrently, for the most part, large motor comes before small motor. Big comes before small. Want strong fingers that can hold a pencil? Then that same body needs to have previously had lots of time in an outdoor environment learning to negotiate where it was in space, how to run, climb, kick, and spin. Preferably barefooted.

Be patient with yourself. If you find you need to recalibrate your own understanding of the importance of playing outside, take the time to do so. Keep an extra sweater, sunglasses, or gloves on hand so you can take care of your needs in order to better meet those of the children! Limiting outdoor play because of *your* discomfort is not acceptable. So whether it be the weather (ha—see what I did there!), clothes, drifting away from DAP, or bugs, everyone needs to take some time to identify barriers to outdoor play and KNOCK THEM DOWN!

 BREATHE

As we continue exploring the importance of outdoor play, we want to also make sure that the outdoor environment is seen as an extension of the inside one, not separate from it. Everything that is IN could, should, and would also be OUT! Blocks build differently when they are on grass or in sand than they do on a perfectly flat, carpeted floor. Sunlight and shadows play with your easel paper in a different manner when you are outside versus being inside. You can draw Really Big Things on the driveway with chalk when you are out. The outdoors is the perfect place for rolling tires, climbing on cable spools, jumping off straw bales, and stacking rocks. You can grow bigger sunflowers outside. No one worries about the ooblick on the floor when you are out. I have always found lunch to taste better when eaten outside, and I guarantee someone would rather listen to you read a story outside on a blanket under a tree than inside on a carpet under the fluorescents. Puzzles and manipulatives can be brought outside, and dress-up clothes can be worn out there too! And while swings, slides, and climbing structures serve their purpose, please be aware that sand, water, gardens, blocks, wild places, loose parts, bikes, and the occasional organized game have been suggested to be possibly *better than* (emphasis mine) fixed equipment when it comes to promoting physical, social-emotional, language and literacy, and cognitive development.

Some of you lucky ducks are fortunate to have a yard that is already stocked with blocks, books, dress-up clothes, loose parts, sandboxes, and other bits of outdoor goodness. Some of you have to load up the wagon and schlep it out each day. I know it's a pain. KEEP DOING IT! Bev Bos used to say that when you are doing what is right and best for children, you will often feel like you are the only one doing it. Do it anyway. And by the way, if someone is telling you that you are *not* allowed to bring things out into the yard, you need to explore this. WHY can't things go outside? Who told you that? Is it really a rule at your program? Or is it one person's preference? If Miss Poopy Face tries to convince you that there are RULES to follow, ask to see them. Do your homework and (politely) ask questions before automatically just caving in. Stop assuming that people are right just because they are older than you, more experienced than you, sound confident, or have a suit on.

My other suggestion is to become a little more familiar with the forest school movement, sometimes called *nature-based schools, nature schools, forest kindergartens*, or *outdoor schools*. Popular in Europe since the 1950s, they have recently begun popping up in the US, so you might or might not be familiar with them. Regardless, my suggestion is to take a page out of the book these guys are writing. Seriously. In the US outdoor play is currently experiencing what I have started calling a *continuum stretch*. At one far end, we have programs that don't even have recess, and over at the other end we see programs where the children are outside, every day, all day, regardless of the weather. This is quite different than your average child care center, elementary school, or family child care home that has some form of daily access to a playground, park, or backyard but still finds themselves somewhere in the middle of this outdoor play continuum. Forest schools themselves have their own continuum; varying *degrees* of forest schools if you will, ranging from programs that have really really long outdoor play sessions *and* a traditional brick-and-mortar building (say, for toileting, napping, storing equipment, and so on) all the way to programs where children are dropped off at the trail head or park entrance with their boots, hats, canteen, flashlight, rope, and machete (that's an exaggeration, but you get my point). I watched a documentary by Lisa Molomot entitled *School's Out: Lessons from a Forest Kindergarten*, where children as young as four years old walked independently from their home to the bus stop, rode the bus solo, and exited the bus at the appropriate stop, where, after being collected by the teacher and classmates, they all walked the rest of the way to their outdoor classroom together.

What these programs share, regardless of their spot on the forest school continuum, is a hard-and-fast belief that children need to be engaged in playful learning outdoors, so they spend most, if not *all*, of the day outside in nature. So while it might be true that what I am presenting in this book may be more geared for folks who are in traditional early childhood settings with *some* amount of outdoor play on a daily basis with children, those of you already spending large amounts of time outside will hopefully receive affirmation of that choice. To the rest of you, I lovingly remind you that you don't need a *forest* to embrace the ideology of a forest school.

One of the best books I ever purchased was *The Developmental Benefits of Playgrounds*, published by the Association for Childhood Education International and written by Joe Frost, Pei-San Brown, John A. Sutterby, and Candra D. Thornton. After I read this book, I wrote a book report on it and posted that to my website and to my Facebook page. Shortly thereafter, it came to my attention that a preschool in California that had been getting pressured to eliminate recess in their program because "they won't get it next year" used the book and my book report to create a PowerPoint presentation to argue their case as to why they refused to eliminate outdoor play in their program. Their presentation was met with so much success that outdoor play started to be valued not only in the preschool program but in the elementary school too! That, my friends, is advocacy in action!

The Developmental Benefits of Playgrounds challenges the playground industry for being too focused on safety at the expense of free play. The book suggests that statistics surrounding the number of playground injuries are misrepresented reports of preschoolers who were "injured" while on equipment designed for school-agers, improperly designed or installed equipment, or equipment that had inappropriate fall surfacing. Couple this with the fact that children in the United States have such poor upper body strength, you could argue that many playground injuries are not due to the equipment but to children's lack of coordination, balance, and core strength, all of which are by-products of not being allowed to run around in the first place. We claim playground equipment to be dangerous because children fall, yet they fall because we never let them play on the equipment; a physical tragedy of a catch-22 if ever I've seen one.

At this juncture, I am reminded of a few things: (1) "Children are curious, not suicidal," one of my favorite quotes from my podcast cohost, Jeff Johnson, (2) "Safety second!" a quote by Heather Shumaker, author of *It's OK to Go Up the Slide*, and (3) the book *Play's Place in Public Education for Young Children* edited by Victoria Jean Dimidjian, specifically chapter four, which addresses the importance of risk-taking and its link to literacy in that children who do not take risks do not become fluent readers. This sentiment is repeated in Jarrod Green's book *I'm OK!*

Building Resilience through Physical Play, where he reminds us that (and I'm paraphrasing) the apprehension children feel when they face a new vocabulary word or a math problem is the same feeling as when they are on a big rock wondering what will happen if they jump off. They can't do either without confidence. Children who have had the opportunity to develop confidence in the rock scenario are more likely to face the math or reading challenge with the same "I can do it" attitude.

The outdoor environment is more conducive to developmentally appropriate risk-taking experiences. But here is more evidence of the catch-22 we find ourselves in; we know preschool-age children need certain kinds of large-motor equipment and activities for optimal physical development, yet many of these same pieces of equipment (think seesaws, jungle gyms, merry-go-rounds) and actions (climbing, running, jumping, throwing) are banned (or are *perceived* to be banned) from schools and child care centers. How do we provide natural, engaging places for recess and other forms of spontaneous free play without fear of litigation directing our efforts? Safety is important, opportunities for developmentally appropriate risk-taking are more so. Why? Because lack of risk in the play environment leads to a generation of children who are either risk averse, never learning how to navigate everyday situations, or are risk seekers, who grow up looking for risks because they never got to experience them as children. And when you are sixteen years old, sliding down a metal slide buck naked on wax paper, or swinging on your tummy, or going UP the slide just isn't going to cut the mustard.

Physical activity leads to higher cognitive functioning. But physical activity is more than sitting on the bench, waiting in line, or waiting for a turn during a once-a-week gym class. "But we don't want them to get hurt!" To which I respond, they are going to get hurt at some point whether you want them to or not!! Lady Allen of Hurtwood, one of the earliest supporters of the adventure playground movement, said, "It is better to risk a broken leg than a broken spirit." A bone will mend. A child's spirit? That's trickier business. No one is suggesting we put children in harm's way, we are advocates for developmentally appropriate risk-taking experiences that are an organic part of playful learning. Adults who work with children must be familiar with the difference between hazards and risks. A *hazard* is something a child might not see that could cause harm, such as cat poop in the sandbox, a nail sticking out of the climbing structure, broken glass in the grass. And for what it's worth, *common sense*, not a policy, is what leads me to remove them and/or point them out to children playing in a certain area. But a *risk* is a situation where a child might not be sure of the outcome, so she finds herself in a situation where she needs to assess her physical and emotional ability to navigate the situation at hand; for example, jumping over a stream, maneuvering through an obstacle course, or attempting to climb a tree. But aye, there's the rub! In order to be able to assess her ability, she needs to have had practice. And that means not only having lots of *time*, but also being around adults who are diligently navigating the balance between developmentally appropriate risks that are a part of playful learning and serious hazards that could cause serious injuries. And for that to happen, we need to stop hovering and insisting on wrapping children in bubble wrap.

As I type (no joke, it JUST happened in front of my eyes outside my window), two eighth-grade girls (my neighbors) noticed a ball in the pine tree out front. (FYI, this ball has been stuck up there for eons). The one threw her shoe up to get it (rookie). Of course that didn't work, and now the ball *and* the shoe are about twenty feet up in the tree. Next I see them run in the house and emerge with a kitchen step stool. Not a lot of extra height, but hey, they're headed in the right direction, right?! Now they throw the second girl's shoe because, well, we're four feet closer! No go. Older brother comes out. "HEEEEYYYYYY," they say! "Help! We need the ball, and now the shoes are up, and, and, and . . ." No joke, older brother gets in the car and drives off. The determination of these middle schoolers was worth the game delay (meaning that I stopped writing to watch how all this played out!). They go back in the house. Now, what I know is that my new neighbors are serious DIY-ers, so I am quite sure there's a wicked big serious gargantuan ladder somewhere in that basement, and these girls are old enough to know this. And I was right. They come back out, a little slower now as they are hauling a huge ladder, one of those bendy space-saver ladders where you have to unfold it and click it into place before you climb (know what I'm talking about?). Anyway, they get it set up. One is holding, one is climbing, and they get the shoes and the ball. There was a minor audible screech as something happened, but no one got hurt and no one died and they got the job done. They figured out how to refold it (that's what caused the screech), I complimented them on sticking with the task and following through, not only with the shoe and ball but with the figuring out of the ladder, and we went on with our day.

What was happening as this scene played out? Whereas some eyeballs might see only a potential lawsuit from the landlord *if* one of the girls had fallen off the ladder, my eyes, and probably yours too, saw developmentally appropriate risk-taking, development of executive function skills—working memory ("I know where the ladder is!"), mental flexibility ("I can keep focused on the ball while keeping my balance on the ladder!"), and self-control ("I'd better slow down, I'm climbing too fast")—problem solving, cooperation, teamwork, persistence and stick-with-it-ness (not giving up!), spatial skills (realizing the original ladder was too short and estimating out how far and hard to toss the shoe, which, incidentally, is also physics), and large-motor skills such as stretching, balancing, reaching, jumping, and throwing.

It becomes easier to see things through the second set of eyeballs when we realize the benefits of what we are calling "risky," and for this we look to Ellen Beate Hanses Sandseter, from Norway, who is one of the leading researchers in the area of risky play. She and her colleagues have identified six categories of risky play:

1. *Playing at great heights*, which might include climbing, jumping, balancing, hanging, and perhaps swinging.

2. *High-speed activities* such as swinging, sliding, sledding, running, bike riding, skating, and skiing.

3. Using what might be seen as *"dangerous" tools*, items like ropes or screwdrivers, and specifically cutting tools like knives, saws, and axes.

4. Playing where there might be the *presence of dangerous elements*, such as near cliffs, near or in deep or icy water, and near fire pits.

5. When children engage in *rough-and-tumble* behaviors like wrestling, fencing, or play fighting.

6. When there is *potential to disappear or get lost*, such as playing or exploring alone or being in an unfamiliar environment.

There are multiple benefits of risky play, including the reduction of irrational fears, anxious responses, and phobias, as well as an increase in the ability to self-manage risks as children get older when adults might no longer be present. During risky play, children expose themselves to manageable amounts of risk, learn how to navigate it, keep their wits about them, and, as Peter Gray says, "Come out alive!" Risky play assists children in coping with new situations, increases creativity, allows children to come face-to-face with their own limitations (and abilities!), and provides opportunities to increase spatial and motor skills. Playworker and advocate Marc Armitage encourages us to consider that all play is risky play to some degree, so he cautions us to not consider risky play a "type" of play, like dramatic play or parallel play. "Risky play is not a category," he says, "it's what children do."

And even though most of you probably won't be coming face-to-face with scenarios stemming from children playing *at great heights*, I bet there will still be climbing and swinging. There might not be deep water or cliffs, but there might be rough-and-tumble play. There are elements of risky play both inside and outside in all early childhood programs, so it's important to reflect on how we are reacting and responding to it. We need to make sure we are **not** stopping these things just because we are afraid of what *might* happen.

> Mothers for miles around worried about Zuckerman's swing. They feared some child would fall off. But no child ever did. Children almost always hang onto things tighter than their parents think they will.
>
> —E. B. White, *Charlotte's Web*

And with a nod to Zuckerman, I offer you a few of the physical benefits of *swinging*:

- swaying
- running
- turning
- leg pumping
- pushing
- jumping
- landing
- pectoral muscle development
- rhythm
- balance
- grasping
- hanging upside down (change of visual perspective)

So many benefits, yet they still get taken away. True story: I was out with some friends and their middle-school-age son who announced over dinner, "I said NO to drugs, and in return they took away my swings!"

I'm a fierce advocate of swings on the yard! What else will we see on a child-centered yard that supports playful learning?

- sun and shade (with shade ideally being provided by nature like large tree branches as opposed to plastic, pop-up style covers)
- water
- swings
- easel
- art materials
- roller paintbrushes for water play
- sand
- dirt
- mud
- shrubs
- plants
- sunflowers
- hills
- grass
- curves
- tools
- bikes
- scooters
- woodworking materials

- tin cans
- slides
- wagons
- ramps
- pathways
- balls
- riding toys
- parachute
- Hula-Hoops
- tunnels
- hideouts
- open area
- gardens
- seating
- ladders
- painting tools
- sensory tubs (sand/water tubs)
- sidewalk chalk
- hammock
- cups, scoops, containers, funnels, shovels

- obstacle course materials: think any material or equipment that facilitates directional movement such as a child moving over, on, under, through, behind, down, around . . .

- maybe a "sound wall" with metal things for banging: hubcaps, washboards, old pans, and wooden spoons

- and of course, last but not least, lots and lots of loose parts such as cones, cable spools, tires, gutters, blocks, pine cones, rocks, tree branches and "cookies," scarves, sheets, spools, hay bales, boards, boxes, barrels, tree stumps, logs, rope, shells, sticks, wood, dryer tubing, fabric, milk crates, sheets, blankets, wooden pallets (the list is endless and much of it can be "harvested" on the side of the road or from the dumpster behind Home Depot, shhhhh!)

Now hold on a minute—what's the big deal with loose parts anyway? Some play scholars, including Rusty Keeler, playground designer and author of *Natural Playscapes*, propose that loose parts might be more beneficial for developing a child's lacking upper-body strength than fixed overhead equipment like monkey bars, overhead ladders, track rides, and rings.

Although *loose parts* has only been an early childhood buzzword for about the last five to ten years, the theory of loose parts is not new. In the early 1970s an architect by the name of Simon Nicholson proposed his *theory of loose parts*:

> In any environment, both the degree of inventiveness and cre-
> ativity, and the possibility of discovery, are directly proportional
> to the number and kind of variables in it.

Lately, these variable have become known simply as "loose parts." Loose parts are materials that have more than one way of being used, things that can be carried, lined up, stacked, moved, combined and then used all over again in a totally different way. Loose parts can be used alone or with other materials, there is no right or wrong way to use them because, at their very core, they are intended to facilitate imaginative and creative constructions and designs. Nicholson believed that *everyone* is creative, and that creativity, especially in children, is encouraged when there is access to open-ended materials such as clay, blocks, rocks, and other materials that can be tinkered with, taken apart, and added to the places where they play. Open-ended materials like loose parts provide an unlimited amount of creative opportunities both indoors and out. The more varied the opportunities the more likely it is for the children to remain engaged, and the more engaged they are the longer and deeper the play.

UH-OH! RANT ALERT!

I am currently concerned that the original idea of open-ended, loose parts play with various *found* materials (boxes, cable spools, tires, gutters, milk crates) has turned into more of a "children using the teacher's collection of bits and bobs" (shiny small rocks, shells, glass beads) reality. I think loose parts play facilitates more of a messy, big, loud, some might say dirty or grimy, junky, seedier side of play that is more conducive to an outdoor setting. Not all adults appreciate this. I appreciate the photo-shoot-worthy aesthetic of a Reggio-inspired, loose-parts-focused classroom too. However, these bits and bobs tend to be more small-motor materials, pretty, shiny, neat, and orderly. There needs to be a balance: big and little, indoors and out. Remembering that in both circumstances, if the materials only *occasionally* come out of the cupboard or the shed, and adults are the ones deciding when this happens and directing how and where the materials are used, *and* the adults are more focused on keeping the loose parts safe, organized, and clean, not only has the true meaning of loose parts been lost, but it is also no longer *play*.

END RANT.

Come back with me to the yard and outdoor space! Keep on gathering those loose parts! Harvest them (that means look behind dumpsters)! Go shopping on the side of the road! I give you permission to get in touch with your inner "picker" as you gather up these open-ended parts of childhood that might look like junk to the untrained eye but are better than anything money can buy! Obstacle courses are often an organic outgrowth of a growing collection of outdoor loose parts. Don't worry about gathering the "right" materials or equipment either. Use loose parts that invite children to move their bodies in various directions: over, under, through, up, down, behind, around, forward, sideways, backward, and also crawling, creeping, and climbing! Start with tires, milk crates, tree stumps, and two-by-four-inch wooden boards and you will be good to go.

Be mindful of how the adults are interacting with children in the yard too. A few chapters from now we will unpack the idea of what it means to be a *facilitator*, but for now, let me remind you that it is very possible to be supportive of children's outdoor adventures without having to be smack in the middle of them. Honestly, you do not need to be playing tag with the school-agers unless they invited you and even then, only if you want to. Remember, if it's really *play*, it's freely chosen and you can quit whenever you want. This is the rule for all play, adults included. Children, especially ones in child care settings, have adults all up in their business all day long. Practice stepping back. You can do this without violating ratio rules or compromising supervision requirements. As you practice pulling back, be mindful of "chickens on a fence" syndrome: a bunch of adults standing on the sidelines not really paying attention, not really disengaged, just kind of *there*. Finding the middle ground between "all up in their business" and "chickens on a fence" takes practice! Engaging in what I call *active observation* allows me to stay in the center without being pulled to one extreme or another. I walk around the yard, milling about, listening, looking, noticing and then using these observations to figure out how I might need to redirect, respond to, or facilitate what is unfolding in the yard. What I am *observing* determines my next course of action, not the schedule.

I think we've made a strong case that children need daily opportunities for walking, running, spinning, digging, climbing, swinging, building, thinking, imagining, and being both loud and quiet. The outdoors is an ideal place for all of these things to happen. It has been suggested that the most common and preferred form of risky play by children is *climbing*, so I'd like to explore this activity, and its importance, in a little more depth.

Many of you probably have a climbing structure of sorts, so I'd like to share my thoughts about lifting children to equipment: don't do it. Seriously. Stop. In our misguided efforts in keeping children "safe," we have started placing and lifting them up to equipment. Needing to be placed or lifted means it's probably too big for you, which means you shouldn't be doing it yet. When children get lifted to equipment, they start to think they can do the activity on their own, and this instills a false sense of skill and mastery. Then the child attempts the action on their own and *that's* how we end up with broken wrists and collarbones. Not by having climbing equipment in the first place. Important clarification: if a child can figure out a way to get on top of the huge cable spool without me lifting her, I will *spot* her from now until Tuesday! I will spot them, side-coach them, walk them through it, facilitate, engage in direct instruction while standing right there with them, but I am not going to lift them. Not lifting kids is one of my few noncompromisables and, if you are keeping track, is now the fourth thing I want you to **break up** with.

Consider your playground or yard. Is there anything to climb? Trees? Jungle gym? Rocks? Bales of hay? Every action has an equal and opposite REaction. Take away things to climb, or forbid climbing on things that are there, and children will use what is left to meet their needs. Their need for risk-taking and excitement is so strong that they will use everything and anything they can get their hands on in an effort to get to do all the things their bodies need to do! And as I just mentioned, you know as well as I do that if we don't provide something to climb, they will find something to climb, whether that be a tree, the slide, the "wrong part" of the structure, a pole, hills, big boulders, a table, the couch, bookcases . . .

So let's unpack this a little deeper. **Why do children climb?**

- because stuff (trees, fences, and furniture) is there
- to increase their visual field
- for excitement
- to experience the feeling of accomplishment
- to get close to nature
- to experience basic physics (gravity, inertia, pendulums, optics)
- to overcome physical challenges
- to test abilities
- to show off
- to compete
- to engage in pretend games
- to retrieve objects
- to stimulate kinesthetic perceptions
- to increase vestibular sensations
- because children are designed to climb and have an innate tendency to do so

Do children need to have certain physical skills to climb successfully? Yes. The physical requirements for climbing vary and depend on what is being climbed. **Do children develop certain skills while climbing?** Again, yes. Climbing involves the following:

- Perceptual motor skills: learned abilities relating to body, spatial, and directional awareness

  - *Body awareness*: the ability to discriminate between body parts and an awareness of what the parts can do

  - *Spatial awareness*: the awareness of how much space the body occupies and the ability to move the body through space

  - *Directional awareness*: left/right, up/down, top/bottom, in/out, front/back

- Fitness abilities: power, agility, speed, balance, and coordination

  - *Balance*: the ability to maintain equilibrium while the body is in various positions is greatly influenced by visual, tactile-kinesthetic, and vestibular stimulation. The vestibular system is located in the inner ear. Vestibular stimulation through swinging and climbing plays an important role in balance, posture, coordination, agility, and vision.

- Visual perception skills: While climbing, children develop the ability to perceive *affordances*. Affordances are the footholds and handholds that the climber uses to support the body while climbing.

Summary: So what if instead of saying, "When children **climb**, they are strengthening their large-motor muscles!" (which, while true, let's be honest, is more of a freshman-seminar-101-level rationale), we got really good at jumping right to a masters-501-level response if (and when) the situation calls for it, saying something like this:

> When children **climb**, they are learning how much space their bodies occupy, strengthening their ability to navigate their bodies through space, and associating gross-motor movements with directional understanding. While the specific physical prerequisites for climbing depend on the actual object(s) being climbed, their efforts will require a minimum level of spatial skills, balance, coordination, and agility.

I don't know about you, but all of a sudden it sounds like climbing is Something Very Important that children should be doing! And I know in my heart that if I asked you to, you could buddy up with a colleague and write a similar justification for throwing. Swinging. Spinning. Running.

Outdoor play offers so many seemingly obvious benefits to a child's growth and development that it can be disheartening to constantly feel like we have to prove it. Taking the *time* to trust our abilities to link what is happening during outdoor play to the four domains of developmentally appropriate practice will assist us in showing colleagues, parents, administrators, and the community at large that we DO NOT need to go back indoors because of a misguided belief that something more important is happening inside. The research is compelling and solid; the many benefits of outdoor play can no longer be ignored as doing so could prove to be life-threatening.

3

Children Are Able to Explore the Environment with Few Restrictions, or You Really Don't Need a Lot of Rules

HOW CAN WE CREATE places where children have the freedom to explore with few restrictions? What does that look like? And how could we get there? These are questions I want to answer, but first, I want to share a thought: I wonder whether adults would find it less challenging to create places where children can explore with few restrictions if they were given the same opportunity. What would it look like to *teach* with fewer restrictions? Are we guilty of overregulating children simply because we are overregulated ourselves (often by a group of individuals who have never done the job)? When we feel like we are drowning in a sea of (often) stupid rules and regulations designed to cater to the lowest common denominator—because we continue to let anyone do this work—do we experience some sense of fulfillment as we exert our power over the people who have even less than us? Is it possible that we feel jealous when children don't have lots of restrictions but we do?

Just a thought.

Let's change gears. When I say that the children are able to explore the environment with few restrictions, what does that look like to you? Remember, having few restrictions does not mean anarchy and chaos—we're not planning a *Lord of the Flies* party! From the perspective of a child, here are some examples to consider:

- painting at the easel without being forced to wear a smock
- building with blocks as high as I want—not just up to my waist
- standing up at snack or at lunch without being told I MUST sit down
- climbing UP the slide
- wearing dress-up clothes outside the dress-up center
- engaging in facilitated rough-and-tumble play
- being able to take manipulatives and other materials to other parts of the room
- lying on my back during story time
- bringing inside stuff outside (easel, books, blocks)
- mixing paint colors
- squishing playdough with my belly
- being able to stay with a thing (project, puzzle, thought, activity) until I am done

If I were sitting next to you right now, we'd walk through them together, and we'd talk about your response to each of them one by one. I'd poke around and see if you had any other examples that were relevant specifically to *you*. We'd unpack your reaction, thought, and response and get down to the nitty-gritty layers of why we say NO to things that really, in the big grand scheme of things, don't matter at all. Save your NO for when someone is really about to get hurt.

Start paying attention to how often NO is used in situations where we just *don't like* something or *don't want to be bothered* versus situations where someone may truly be in harm's way. I want you to start asking yourself, "Why did I just stop that behavior? Why did I say NO?"

It is perfectly OK for you to *not like* something a kid does, but *not liking it* is not a valid reason for stopping someone's behavior. I need you to make room for it and to respect it. You don't need to like it, you don't need to "get it," and you surely don't need to want to do it. But please remember that just because *you* don't want to do it doesn't mean it's not worth doing.

Micromanaging the behaviors of small children drains you of all your emotional and physical energy. It makes you tired. And then, later in the day when you come face-to-face with something really important, you are exhausted because you used up all your energy having an ongoing power struggle with McKenzie because *how many times have I told you that the dress-up shoes need to stay in the dress-up center?!*

What is the *worst possible thing* that would happen if she wore the high-heeled shoes as she went over to the manipulative area to get a puzzle? If she wore them over to the sensory tub to pour and mix the colored rice? To the easel to paint a picture? International speaker and author Barbara Coloroso asks her audiences, "Is this life-threatening?" and I just love that. Is someone about to DIE if this continues? And if the answer is no, why do we insist on making it stop? If McKenzie just loves wearing fancy shoes, boas, and beads and the only time she is allowed to do so is when she is in the dress-up area, it makes perfect sense that she resists gentle suggestions to "play somewhere else." So what if instead of daily power struggles we *relaxed* the rule a little bit? Eased up on the restrictions. What if she were able to wear these things as she explores other areas in the room? What might that look like? What would have to happen for us to let it go?

Learning how to say YES instead of always leading with NO is a big part of having fewer restrictions. But learning how to do it takes time! The good news is that, as anyone who has been in this field longer than five years can tell you, we change. We change our minds, our techniques, our understandings. What assists us in doing so? Experiences, mentors, workshops, books, certain children, aha moments, articles, lots of things might contribute. One of the reasons I feel it's OK for me to be as direct as I am in my writing and my workshops is *because I used to do all of this stuff*. Shoot, I have some colleagues who call that time in their career "before we knew better." Of course we are *all* always growing, learning, and changing our minds, but there are also times when we make HUGE LEAPS, like fish-flopping-up-onto-the-shore-and-growing-legs level of change. Like bright light bulbs of "Aha!" and "Eureka!" levels of insight and awareness that definitely changed our practice for good.

Some of my conversations with colleagues about "before we knew better" sound like support group meetings: "Hello, I'm Lisa Murphy, and I used to have a lineup line, a whistle, a rule sheet with twenty-five NO-NO's on it, and a Pinterest-inspired 'Think about It Chair' (a cute code for time-out)!" But we change our minds. Why? For tons of reasons. Maybe the old ways weren't working, maybe we started to realize there were other ways of doing business, maybe someone straight-up told us to STOP IT because it wasn't best practice, maybe we read a book or an article or took a class and discovered that our methods weren't entirely developmentally appropriate.

Regardless of *how* we got to this point, we started thinking about *why* we were saying NO all the time and how attempting to enforce a bunch o' rules meant more for compliance and adult control than for developing self-regulation. Who are these rules for? What purpose do they serve? The questions we began asking eventually led us to a point where we were able to stand up and admit that although we drank the DRESS-UP CLOTHES NEED TO STAY IN THE DRESS-UP CENTER Kool-Aid in the early days of our teaching, it started to leave a sour taste in our mouth. And instead of stubbornly continuing to swallow it because of habit (fixed mind-set), we decided it was time to stretch ourselves and make some changes (growth mind-set).

After years of this kind of self-reflection and questioning, I arrived at a place of having only one rule: *that people are not for hurting.*

Oh, how I can hear the shouts of "But I need to keep them safe!" and "Children need to learn how to follow the rules!" and "It's not always going to be fun and games!" First off, no one is telling you to compromise anyone's safety. Second, who made these rules anyway? Third, are they really rules or are they someone's personal preference? Or, even better, someone's *interpretation* of a rule? And fourth, we also need to consider the not-rules. What's a not-rule? They are the unwritten, inconsistent, mood-driven, "I just need you to stop that," and "because I said so" statements we make, typically when we are tired, stressed, frazzled, and overwhelmed.

"STOP THAT! WE DON'T DO THAT HERE!"

"No?" HIT HIT HIT! "I just did it again!"

"WE DON'T PLAY GUNS AT SCHOOL!"

"It's not a gun, it's a *plane*."

"HANDS ARE NOT FOR HURTING!"

"That's not my hand, it's my *wrist*."

"WE DON'T HIT OUR FRIENDS!"

"She's not my friend!" SMACK!

When we spend a good chunk of our day attempting to enforce what's posted on a rule sheet, our job is reduced to behavior cop. Relationships are compromised, conversations are scrapped, and we spend a lot of time telling children what we *don't* want them doing instead of being clear and consistent with our expectations of what we *do* want. By the way, this is the fifth thing I want you to **break up** with: the habit of telling children what you don't want them to do. Instead, get in the habit of telling them what you want them to do.

This really isn't that difficult; it just takes time. Literally. Am I taking the *time* to think about what is about to come out of my mouth? Am I being clear? Am I trying to enforce a mood-driven demand? (Examples: I have a headache, so I want the block area

> ### Things to Break Up with Review List
>
> twenty-minute time blocks
>
> moving like a herd
>
> asking fake questions
>
> lifting children to equipment
>
> telling kids what we don't want them to do

closed! I just washed those paint cups, so the easel is off-limits right now!) Am I being consistent in my expectations? Am I telling/showing/modeling what I want them to do? Or am I running around all day telling the children what I don't want them to do? Who decided what rules got posted on the wall? And what happens when the posted rules get broken? Bribing? Yelling? Punishment? Shame? Humiliation? Ostracism? Time-out? Moving your clip to red? All of these things compromise relationships.

Let me cut right to the chase: time-out does not work. A child does *not* learn how to be a part of a social group by being isolated. It's true that time-out gives all parties time away from each other, which in certain situations probably isn't a bad thing. In my experience, however, when an adult puts a child in time-out, it is typically the *adult* who needs the break, not the kid. How amazing would it be if ALL teachers realized—regardless of the situation that transpired—that they cannot be effective while in an escalated emotional state??

The other thing I want to say about time-out might be a little bit of a reach, but I'm going to offer it up anyway. If you have not yet broken up with "moving like a herd" and consequently everyone is always having to do everything at the same time and there is no time for independent exploration or solo activities, I'd like to suggest that if I were a child who liked to play dinosaurs or Legos or do activities *by myself* and I have not been allowed to do that all day, I just might start acting up so you will PUT me in time-out simply so I can sit *by myself* for a few minutes.

And for the love of all things holy! BURN your rainbow-colored, stoplight-format, color-coded behavior charts. Now. I could write an entire article on this (but Travis Manlay already did), so I'm going to sum it up in one phrase: *stop the public shaming*. According to Manlay, these charts teach children three things: (1) be compliant so the teacher will love you, (2) be compliant so you can be like the "good" kids, and (3) be compliant so you don't get ratted out. I don't care how "cute" the font is or how many "likes" the picture you posted of it on Instagram got, these charts have nothing to do with behavior management and everything to do with an adult's need for control. What if we posted one in the teacher break room and subjected teacher performance to such public humiliation?

Recently at a gig in Nebraska, I asked how they'd like it if one was posted in the break room. Then—without them knowing what I was doing—I started in with some improv in response to things that were actually happening (they seemed a willing crowd!).

"Hey! You're late! Move your clip!"

"Hey! You're on your phone! Move your clip!"

"Hey! Where are you going? I think you've used the bathroom enough today, sit back down, but first, move your clip!"

"Hey! No talking! Move your clip!"

"Hey! Eyes on me! Move your clip!"

No joke, their eyes BULGED and they looked scared. And they are adults! I could tell that a few of them were processing. Like big time! Like, "Dayum, this feels horrible! I am so embarrassed. Why is she hollering? I feel so belittled!" I asked them how they felt. They said, "Horrible!"

Exactly. Stop it.

I have never concealed the fact that I loathe these things, but my level of disdain escalated this past summer when I was at a conference and there was a vendor selling one that I had never seen before. Now I'm sure you've all seen the green light (good!), yellow light (caution!), red light (bad!) chart styles. The one I saw at the conference was different. This one had five levels:

1. SUPERHERO

2. GAINING POWER

3. HERO

4. LOSING POWER

5. POWERLESS

Everyone started at HERO in the morning. The rest of the day? Well . . .

Charts like this do not teach self-regulation, they mandate compliance. There is a difference. While some will argue and insist that children are *choosing* to not follow the rules, I'd also like to remind everyone that they are four. Additionally, I'll counterargue that most of the rules those same four-year-olds are expected to follow are silly. I'd also state that as a four-year-old, if I am being told on a regular basis that I'm *powerless*, at some point I'm going to start believing it. We might as well dump ice-cold buckets of water on their heads. Or reinstate corporal punishment. Teachers cringe at the thought of such physical punishment yet continue to dole out emotional punishment on a daily basis. These outdated and inappropriate methods are long overdue for retirement.

We claim to want high levels of executive function and self-regulation skills, but for that to happen, children need long periods of uninterrupted free time for playing inside and out so they can practice making choices and figuring out how to develop relationships with each other; *this* is the recipe for high levels of self-regulation, not color-coded charts with clips that do more harm than good.

 BREATHE

So what would it take to throw the time-out chairs in the trash and burn the behavior charts? What would it look like if the rules started to change and modify to become more flexible, realistic, and developmentally appropriate? What if we started making sure that our expectations were aligned with DAP and child development theory and ages and stages instead of a one-size-fits-all posted set of rules designed to CONTROL the children? It might be *easier* to have a posted rule sheet that tells us what IS and is NOT acceptable, just as it is *easier* when we have a minute-by-minute dictated daily schedule. But it's only *easier* because it's saving us the messy business of having to think. Good teaching isn't *easy*. Good teaching is relevant and meaningful, and that takes hard work.

So, to repeat, I have one rule: people are not for hurting. We deal with everything else as it comes up. How can this be possible, to have only one rule? The quick-and-dirty answer to this question is because the *secret* to good teaching is controlling the environment, not the children in it. I honestly believe this is such a simple concept that we overthink it and make it harder than it needs to be. But seriously, and I mean this with every ounce of sincerity in my body, if you remember nothing other than this *secret* after reading the book (and spend some time figuring out how to put it into action), you will be on the right track. And after a little bit of time, you will come to realize that you really *don't* need a forty-nine point rule sheet, a time-out chair, or a stoplight chart. You will never again need to attend another classroom or behavior management workshop because you will have seen with your own eyes the subtle yet drastic difference between controlling the environment and controlling a child, which is at the heart of why you no longer need so many rules.

Follow me to the next chapter where we will unpack this *secret* a little bit more.

4

The Secret to Good Teaching, or Controlling the Environment Instead of the Children

YEARS AGO I was paired up with a teacher who had forty-nine rules posted on the wall of her preschool classroom. Not only did all of the rules start with the word "NO" she also had them memorized by number so if you were messing around she could yell out the number of the rule you were violating and send you to the office: "Five! Out!" "Ten! Out!" "Seven! Out!" Upon arriving at the office, the children were asked, "Why are you here?" and in between sobs they'd say, "I'm (sob) here for (sob) number ten (sob)." They were asked, "What is number ten?" to which they would cry out, "I don't know, (sob) (sob) I can't read!"

Walls filled with rule sheets filled with NO-NO's that no one can read is an effort at controlling the children instead of the environment and is the complete *opposite* of what defines good teaching. I told you in the last chapter that I have only one rule: that people are not for hurting. I am able to do this because I control the *environment*, not the children.

Many of the rule sheets I come across are a standard-issue list of classroom NO-NO's:

NO hitting

NO screaming

NO biting

NO throwing

NO yelling

NO running

NO NO NO NO NO . . .

How do we start moving away from this?

CAUTION! Please remember that this is a process! Honor it! Going back to the classroom and ripping down the rule sheet, thinking, "Lisa said I don't need this!" will not work. Reflecting leads to realizations that lead to changes that will be long term and way more effective. It's the same as when you investigated the evolution of the daily schedule a couple of chapters back: it's all about reflecting, not reacting. I'd honestly rather have you in your classroom being all business as usual, even if that means having a poster of twenty-five rules, *IF* (and I do mean *IF*) at the same time you are now intentionally reflecting on what it means to control the environment instead of the children. Baby steps!

That being said, our first order of business is making peace with the fact that each and every one of these behaviors is, in actuality, developmentally appropriate yet socially unacceptable. Read that again. Developmentally appropriate yet socially unacceptable. Part of our job as early childhood people is to assist children in learning how to navigate certain social expectations (read: become socially acceptable) while respecting where they are developmentally. That being said, while it is 100 percent developmentally appropriate for young children to hit, bite, kick, run, throw, and scream, it doesn't mean we make some grand announcement that they are ALLOWED to do it. I'm not going to say, "Welcome to Ms. Lisa's room! You are allowed to bite here!" However, when it happens (and it will), no one freaks out, overreacts, and goes all bonkers, because we accept that children bring these behaviors to the table. I think we often forget what children can and cannot do. There is no shame in blowing the dust off your Child Development 101 textbook and giving yourself a reminder of the behavioral expectations of the ages and stages in your program. A main cause of frustration in classrooms, which leads to more attempts by the adult to control the *child*, is the disconnect between an adult expectation (don't knock the blocks over!) and the developmental age/stage of the child (but I'm two!).

Reality check: You can spray-paint the words NO BITING! on the wall in a toddler room. What is still going to happen? Exactly, biting. Because they are rotten little monsters? NO!!! Because they are toddlers and that is part of what they do! Running around, pointing at the sign, telling them WE DON'T DO THAT HERE! is a waste of your energy. Additionally, they get to witness your (over)reaction to the behavior, and what happens next? We get an *entire room* full of biting because of how you initially responded to it! Some of the best advice I have ever received as a teacher was given to me years ago by Dan Hodgins when he said to me, STOP MAKING MORAL ISSUES OUT OF DEVELOPMENTAL ONES. Might this be another thing to **break up** with? Perhaps. (And it is number six if you are keeping track.)

I promise that taking Dan's advice will assist you in your efforts to minimize the restrictions in your classroom and really start understanding what it means to control the environment instead of the children. Please please please save the *how much it hurts* and *friends don't bite* and *would you want me to do that to you* moral monologue for another day. Reframe it. Focus only on the *verb*. For one quick second, see the behavior without the moral lens. What's the verb? In this example, the verb is *biting*. Focus ONLY on the verb

> ### Things to Break Up with Review List
>
> twenty-minute time blocks
>
> moving like a herd
>
> asking fake questions
>
> lifting children to equipment
>
> telling kids what we don't want them to do
>
> making moral issues out of developmental ones

(not character judgements) as you redirect with a calmly stated, "You need to do some biting. People are not for biting. Come, let's find something that you can bite."

That's it. Simple. Done. No screaming. No shaming.

UH-OH! RANT ALERT!

Some things for your consideration that should go without saying. First: Watch for patterns and get in there *before* the bite happens. Early childhood educators are always paying attention because young children COMMAND and REQUIRE you to be constantly observing. This doesn't mean hovering on top of them and being all up in their business (they are practicing autonomy too), it means you are diligently scanning the room and paying attention. If you think children "should know better," you need to read (or reread) your Child Development 101 textbook or consider a new career.

Second: Be diligent in modeling language for *all* of the children in the room. Just as we remind kids that people are not for biting, we are also empowering others to learn how to say "DON'T BITE ME!"

Third: Be mindful of not being too overly dramatic with either child. This means not being overly sappy and goo-goo gaga with the one who got bit or overly harsh with the other. Remaining emotionally neutral and maintaining a matter-of-fact attitude in these situations is challenging. It gets easier when you start to see the behavior as developmentally appropriate instead of a child "being mean."

Fourth: Do Not Label. *See the child, not just the behavior.* Don't slip down the seductive slope of now referring to this child as a biter. I heard a workshop presenter lovingly remind her audience that *sometimes a bite is a hug gone awry*, a hello that took a wrong turn. This is sound advice. Be aware of how you *see*, and subsequently *judge*, the behavior of young children.

END RANT! Not really—I want you to go back and reread the RANT, but this time substitute the word HIT for BITE.

Do it again and plug in THROW.

Remember I am encouraging you to reframe the behavior, to see the *verb* without any attached moral judgements. What I am *not* doing is suggesting that you should begin telling kids TO throw or TO hit. I want you to redirect them. How can the *verb* happen in a way where people don't get hurt? This is learning how to control the environment instead of the children.

"You need to do some *throwing*. There are balls outside and beanbags over here. Which would you like to throw?"

"You want to do some *hitting*, here are some pillows. Put them on the couch and hit them until you are done."

CAUTION! Examples such as these are only effective once you have decided that this is how you are going to handle things FROM NOW ON! This is why baby steps and reflecting (not *reacting*) are all so very important. If you just read this chapter and then think, "Lisa said it's OK to hit pillows, I need to go buy some pillows," you have not thought it through. Kids are going to sense your hesitancy. They are going to be hitting pillows, throwing pillows, chewing on pillows, jumping on pillows because they are going to be wondering (whether they articulate it or not), "Is this how it is now? Can I hit this pillow whenever I need to? Today? Tomorrow? Next week? OR DID YOU READ A BOOK AND NOW YOU THINK LISA MURPHY IS CRAZY AND YOU'RE ABOUT TO REACH YOUR BREAKING POINT AND CHANGE YOUR MIND AND TAKE THE PILLOWS AWAY?!"

Reframing is only effective if it is consistent and not mood dependent, and redirecting is only effective if it actually happens. Please elaborate, Lisa: If I say, *calmly* and *without clenched teeth* (because remember, we are working on no longer making MORAL issues out of developmental ones), "Hey, the room is too small to throw blocks inside. We can set up a throwing station outside if you can wait, or there is a laundry basket (or an empty box) and beanbags (or balled-up socks) right here if you cannot . . ."

. . . and there really *are* balls or sticks or rocks to throw outside AND the transition to get out there isn't too long from now AND/OR the laundry basket (or boxes) and beanbags (or balled-up socks) are always in the room, this "behavior problem" is probably going to deescalate and there's a good chance it might disappear.

. . . but if we never really get to go outside, and the beanbags are in the closet in the teacher room, and you are here by yourself so you can't go get them, and the laundry basket is being used to store jackets, or if I have been conditioned to realize that you might change your mind, or take the blocks away if I forget that you asked me to wait, I am still going to be a pain in your ass and you will think that I am THAT KID: the problem child who doesn't follow the rules.

Our own inconsistency leads to more attempts to control the children instead of the environment.

In my workshops I tell you that if you *don't* want the children to touch it, smell it, taste it, fiddle with it, lose it, break it, hide it, hoard it, stack it, pour it, lick it, it shouldn't be in the room! We laugh at how simple this sounds and nod in agreement to the statement, yet how many of us spend a good chunk of the day trying to control a child's behaviors when the environment could be doing the redirecting for you???

Think about this for a minute.

If you put bowls, wooden spoons, flour, salt, food coloring, a pitcher of water, and an electric mixer on the table because you are about to make a batch of playdough and actually think young kids aren't going to mess with all of it, you are going to be in for a rude awakening! *Your* expectation is out of line, not the children's behavior. They are not being disobedient, you put out a table full of exciting stuff! Stuff that invites *touching*—it's screaming TOUCH ME! Now you find yourself trying to control the kids (don't touch it!) instead of initially controlling the environment (leaving stuff on the counter until you were ready to do the project).

What other *invitations* are the children being given that maybe we've just never noticed?

the runway in the middle of the room (run!)

the glue bottle (squeeze!)

the toilet bowl (splash!)

the basket of tennis balls (bounce! throw!)

the books (rip! tear!)

the stair-step bookcase (climb!)

The child needs to (verb) . They saw an opportunity to (verb) using (material/object) because the (material/object) sent an invitation to do so.

Let's review! *Identifying the invitations leads to isolating the verb, which leads to no longer making moral issues out of developmental ones, which leads to controlling the environment, not the children, which is ultimately what allows for fewer rules and restrictions.*

By taking a minute to reframe and redirect, I am practicing how to *reflect* on behaviors instead of *reacting* to them. How often do we spend time trying to manage behaviors that only came about because of environmental invitations? By controlling the environment instead of the children we are able to start saying YES more. Not yes because we are afraid to tell children NO, but YES because we have gotten rid of the NO-NO's. How do we start moving toward a more YES-YES place instead of remaining in a NO-NO one?

NO is not a bad word. However, just like I said in the previous chapter, I want you to start paying attention to how often you use it and in what context. The word NO stops the action. We say STOP SQUEEZ-ING THE GLUE when the bottle is clearly inviting the behavior. I'm repeating myself, but I'm not apologizing for it because it's important: isolate the behavior and focus on the verb. The child is showing you that they need to *squeeze*. Instead of overreacting in an attempt to control the child with demands of "STOP SQUEEZING!", look at the environ-ment and figure out a way for *squeezing* to happen! I'm still going to provide glue, but in a manner that doesn't *invite* squeezing. At the same time, I'm going to wrangle up some recycled dish-soap bottles and set them near the water table for children to *squeeze* until the cows come home. I am NOT saying the kids should be able to use all the glue because of a desire to squeeze; I'm saying it's on *us* as the adults to figure out how to facil-itate the need for the squeezing. Those who think I'm encouraging children to waste glue are completely missing the point.

Figuring out how to control the environment instead of the children requires you to deal with your own control issues, values, and expecta-tions, and that is challenging, hard,

Squeezing is a very important action for young children. Squeezing facilitates fine-motor development, so if you wanted to get technical, squeezing water out of recy-cled dish-soap bottles for a good part of the morning can be classified as a prewriting exercise.

emotional work! And anyone who tells you it's not is selling something. Once we begin examining the onion that is our "stuff" we often quickly discover that there are waaaaaay more layers to our onion than we thought! We may find ourselves face-to-face with expectations that were put on us when we were little, which we now put on the children we work with. We expect from them what was expected from us—Sit still! Don't run! Be nice! No talking!—and because of this, we try to control the children instead of the environment.

To get really good at controlling the environment instead of the children, you must do whatever is necessary to unpack what you bring to the table. Moral stances? Values? Expectations? Issues? Whatever word works as you allow yourself to identify them, I call them "isms." Everyone has them. Buttons that trigger irrational responses. Kids can sniff 'em out within sixty seconds of meeting you! Children become master poker players at this juncture and can spot your "tell" within seconds! Hate it when kids pick their nose? Tap you on the leg? Rock in their chair? Hum while eating? Put their shirts on backward? Cling to you like Velcro? Follow you around all day? Attempt to get your attention by repeating, "Teacher? Teacher? Teacher?" while patting your hand at the same time? Put their shoes on the wrong feet? They'll be doing it within minutes. But only when YOU are in the room. Not your coteacher. Know why? She has her own set of triggers. Children are brilliant observers.

One of the suggestions I have for all of you reading this book is to spend some time defining, investigating, pondering, unpacking (whatever words work for you) the idea of CONTROL versus STRUCTURE. Being child centered means there is structure, boundaries, and, among other things, consistency. What has been intentionally reduced and removed is the adult's need/desire/attempt to control the children. With this in mind, when folks say to me, "We really like what you said at the workshop today, Lisa, but our program is a lot more *structured* . . ." nine times out of ten, when gently pushed, what they are calling *structure* is actually *control*. Even a quick, nonscholarly Google search will shed light on basic differences. STRUCTURE brings up words and phrases such as having a plan, organization, a model to guide decisions, to construct or arrange according to a plan, give a pattern or organization to. Google

CONTROLLING and not only do you get phrases like being in charge, to determine the behavior, to direct/manage/supervise, to command and dominate, you also get links to pages that address how a controlling personality can lead to the development of toxic relationships.

Needing CONTROL means I need you to do it my way. Even worse, "my way" could change depending on the MOOD I am in, so how I want it done can be different day by day, hour by hour. This can lead to a very confusing atmosphere for our coworkers and children alike. I continue to wonder why adults assume the program will collapse into chaos if they aren't the boss of things.

STRUCTURE means there's organization and consistency. My mood is not a variable. I once talked with a gentleman on a plane who said that "back in the day" kids were given a wide berth when it came to playing around with friends outside, but the structure was SET IN STONE. The boundaries (he used a fence analogy) didn't really ever change and because of this stability, predictability, and consistency, children had the ability to freely explore within the boundaries of the fence. But when those streetlights came on, your butt better be back home. The fence remained the same. Kids weren't distracted by random, erratic, unpredictable changes to the fence. This allowed them the freedom to go about the business of being kids WITHIN THE ESTABLISHED STRUCTURE.

Freedom within the structure. Minimal restrictions. Lots of time to explore both inside and out. Children need adults who are willing to bring these ingredients to the environment, not their control issues. Perhaps the difference between controlling a child and controlling the environment and, by extension, starting to see the subtle differences between structure and control might be explained more effectively through a couple of real-life scenarios. So go pour yourself the beverage of your choice—we'll wrap up this chapter with story time.

Scenario 1: The Shoe Bucket

I believe that children have the right to experience the textures that are available in their environment with their bare feet—if they desire. Being barefoot is an important activity. It reduces stress, aids in developing balance, and provides various opportunities for sensory exploration. The issue in this specific scenario was that my licensing agent didn't want the children in the child care center to be barefoot for any reason at any time. She was anxious not only about shoes and socks being all over the place (give me some credit, for crying out loud!) but also about that *fire* that everyone seems so worried about. Let's break this down. Desiring and/or attempting to have children keep their shoes on all day is an example of needing CONTROL. Jumping to the conclusion that shoes and socks would be strewn all over the place is an example of not TRUSTING me and of assuming that being child centered is a chaotic land mine of a tripping hazard.

How did we reframe it? I pointed out that we provided a bucket for shoes. It literally was a plastic tub that restaurants use for bussing tables. Big enough to contain shoes and socks, small and light enough to be picked up and handled by a child. It was typically always in the same location (structure). No one made grand announcements to children, YOU ARE ALLOWED TO TAKE YOUR SHOES OFF HERE!!! (that is *instigating*, and we'll get to that in the next chapter), but when a child self-initiated the behavior, no one freaked out. We introduced the child to the expectation, which was consistent and not driven by anyone's mood. Read: structure. The environment was controlled, not the children. Want to take off your shoes? Great! Here's what happens: Take off your shoes, take off your socks, put your socks inside your shoes, and put the shoes in the box. When you are done being barefoot, repeat the process—in reverse.

McKenzie was the boss of the shoe bucket in the (un)likely event there was a real or practice fire drill. If the fire-drill bell went off McKenzie (we called her MackADoo) knew she was to get the bucket while the teacher grabbed the roster and emergency prep bag, then we would all gather at the exit door, counting heads as we walked out, and then proceed to meet up with the other classes at the designated fire-drill meet-up location.

Freedom within the structure means there is a consistent system for if and when you want to take your shoes off. This is controlling the environment. Much different than trying to make sure no one ever takes their shoes off! Which is an attempt to control the children.

Scenario 2: Standing Up at Circle

Scene: I am reading to a group of children on the carpet. Someone decides they want to stand up for the duration of the story. CONTROL over the kids means I want all of the children sitting down crisscross applesauce, "one, two, three, eyes on me" while I'm reading, so in response to this behavioral infraction, I can (a) stop reading and announce to the air that I would like everyone to sit down and then I'll keep reading, (b) stop reading and point out how much I loooooooove how Laura Anne is sitting nicely on her bottom, or (c) directly tell the stander-upper to sit back down.

A less controlling response would be to simply make note that it happened and then wait to see what (if anything) transpires. What I don't do is assume that it is going to be a problem. When adults constantly view classroom scenarios with a "this might turn into a problem" lens, they project their own stuff onto the situation, are already mentally trying to solve a problem they don't even have (which is mentally waaaay more exhausting than people realize), and might be inadvertently modeling to the other children that they should see potential conflict too.

I don't assume that "Kayla can't see the book" just because Jonathon is standing up. Why don't I do this? Because I have no data to prove my assumption to be true. She hasn't told me she can't see it. Maybe she doesn't need to see the pictures. Maybe she is futzing with a loose string on the carpet and is listening to the story while messing around with the string and doesn't necessarily neeeeeed to see the book. So again, I don't assume there's a problem where there might not be one. I am *aware* of each variable playing out on the carpet while I am reading the story (versus being oblivious to them), but I resist the urge to jump in and take CONTROL of it. There's no need.

Some view my response to scenarios such as this as though I'm letting a child "get away with something," but let's break it down. There is room for Jonathon to be responsive when reasonable requests are made of him, sure. There is also room for Kayla to learn to take the initiative and either state what her problem might be, or, perhaps get up and change where she is sitting so as to get a better view of the book. It is NOT on me—nor is it my job—to *assume* that Kayla has a problem with Jonathon's action of standing up. Nor do I want to accidentally train her (or other kids for that matter) to think there should be one by immediately jumping in and telling Jonathon to move over or sit down. Me having an issue with something doesn't necessarily mean the other person's behavior has to change. Who is actually having the problem here?

Now, if Kayla suddenly announces that she can't see, I have a couple options, but out the gate I'm not going to jump to any conclusions or make any assumptions. This is the plan, the structure, the consistent variable—to not overreact and to not think children MUST BE SITTING DOWN (that is trying to control the children). I'm a big fan of incorporating reflective listening in my work with children, so after Kayla states that she can't see, I might simply repeat back to her what I heard, "You can't see from where you are sitting." And see where that goes. She might initiate standing up and moving. She might now see the "obstacle" and ask Jonathon to please move over. Who knows, Jonathon might turn around and realize that he IS in the way and scoot over himself! Controlling the environment in this case means moving to where you can see instead of having assigned places on the carpet come hell or high water and by golly we aren't going to proceed until everyone's bottoms are on the floor. That would be controlling the child.

The long and short of it is that I have broken up with my need for CONTROL and compliance simply because I am the adult. And specific to this scenario, I have decided to never ever deny children the opportunity to negotiate, communicate, or problem solve with each other just so I can get to the end of the book!

Scenario 3: Eating the Playdough

One year I had a little guy in my class named Curtis who absolutely loved eating playdough. And not just eating it, but licking it, licking his hands after playing with it, the whole kit and caboodle. And when adults hollered out, "CURTIS! Don't eat the playdough!" know what happened? Yep! He kept eating the playdough! Why? Because he was constantly being told what he couldn't do (eat it!) instead of what he could do (roll it, squish it, cut it, mash it!). The adults were trying to control HIM and his behavior instead of the environment. So what did we do? I made him a batch of eating playdough. We kept it in his cubby and I told him that it was the playdough for eating. The playdough on the table was for squeezing, stretching, rolling, and cutting, and if he wanted to eat it, he needed to eat the dough we now kept in his cubby. A perfect example of controlling the environment instead of the child. The structure component here is that Curtis now had consistent access to the "eating playdough" in his cubby, and I wasn't going to change my mind tomorrow and take it away and put him in time-out instead. Want to eat it? Knock yourself out, but THAT is the playdough for eating (in your cubby) and THIS is playdough for playing (on the table).

And guess what happened to the behavior after about a week? Yep. It stopped. Whereas threats and commands would've done nothing other than add fuel to the fire, which would've led to nothing other than a good old-fashioned power struggle and, as my ex-husband used to say, the kids will always win a power struggle because at the end of the day, adults just want it quiet. So there ya go.

Scenario 4: Activity Time

Freedom within STRUCTURE might mean that from ten a.m. to eleven-thirty a.m., we are all inside the classroom and the children are free to select and engage with any of the materials they see, including but not necessarily limited to blocks, dress-up, math/manipulatives, coloring/markers, Legos, easels, playdough, books, or the sensory tub. Part of this time a Teacher Planned Thing might be happening at the blue table. However, the Teacher Planned Thing is an option, just like everything else in the space. A more CONTROLLING mind-set is that because it is ten a.m., everyone needs to be at the table doing the project I have planned and the other parts of the room are "closed" until I announce they are "open," and I attempt to make each child "do" a project instead of seeing the value of facilitating choice.

Scenario 5: Walking Down the Hallway

What if instead of trying to control children's bodies and voices with bribes and threats as they walk down the hallway to the playground we put the youngest children closer to the exit door? Just a thought. #snarky

Scenario 6: Standing While Eating

I think after reading the previous five you probably could write this one yourself. Sometimes there are a few kids who want to eat standing up. This doesn't mean running around the room with a carrot or a sandwich hanging out of their mouths. It means "I simply don't want to sit while eating." A CONTROL mind-set expects children to sit down! Now! Similar to the shoe bucket scenario, a space that provides few restrictions and is controlling the environment instead of the children might reframe this situation as such: If you want to eat standing up, first move your chair against the wall, then eat, then clear your spot, then move your chair back, then go get ready for nap (or whatever your postlunch routine may be). This is yet another example of freedom within the consistent STRUCTURE.

Let's break it down, why do chairs get moved? Because it's on me to remove hazards (these are things the child potentially might *not* see), such as the *chair* they forget is behind them as they get into an animated conversation about what happened in the sandbox earlier that morning. I am not assuming they are going to lose their balance and fall over, I am removing the possibility of it. I am controlling the environment. Additionally, I am removing any fuel a naysayer (or disagree-er, pick your poison) can obtain if, in fact, a child *does* fall over, causing the naysayer to feel entitled to say, "See! It *is* dangerous! No one is allowed to stand up at lunch anymore!"

With an overarching goal of deepening relationships and encouraging conversations, quite honestly, whether a child sits or stands while eating is not the hill I'm going to die on. And this is just how it is here, Monday through Friday. The adult's *mood* doesn't dictate if the behavior is OK today or not. Please notice that in all of these scenarios there is still structure, predictability, organization, and routine. There is also the gift of *time*, both for me as the teacher and for the children as well. Because my day is not ruled by the clock or a posted rigid schedule, I don't feel pressure to hurry toward a resolution or solution just to stay on task. I never deprive children of the opportunity to talk with each other, problem solve, or negotiate. The only thing missing in these scenarios is the adult's insistence on everything being done their way. Relinquishing our need to control the children is a huge part of being child centered.

5

Adults Serve as Facilitators within the Space

REMEMBER THE TEACHER with the forty-nine rules posted on the wall? The teacher I was paired up when I first started teaching? She had waaaay too many rules and waaaaay too many age-inappropriate expectations of a room full of three-year-olds. She had masking tape lineup lines, whistles, and a key around her neck. This key opened the cupboard and in the cupboard was all the stuff. And the stuff only came out when she was in a good mood. No exaggeration, whenever she would walk toward the cupboard, the kids would go crazy with anticipation of what might be coming out! They'd be giggling among themselves, looking back and forth at each other, wide-eyed and excited. "She's going to the cupboard! She's going to the cupboard!" They would talk in enthusiastic whispers, careful of not being too loud because they didn't want to risk the chance of her locking whatever it was back up again because "some children just weren't ready for something special."

Her need to control the children (versus controlling the environment) prohibited her from being a facilitator, so instead she became the keeper of the stuff. And the stuff was always in the cupboard. And she was the boss of when it all came out. Now here's the thing (using the language from the last chapter): the STRUCTURE component is that I might not have enough space, so I have stuff in cupboards and in the closet. Fine, no biggie. I don't care if you have a cupboard and honestly, I don't care if you keep it locked. I care very much, though, if half a dozen kids come up to you and say, "Please can we bring the sidewalk chalk outside?!" and you say NO for no reason other than that using the chalk wasn't your idea, so now you've decided it's not sidewalk chalk day. That is CONTROL.

Go get the chalk. Or the playdough. Or the flubber. Or the smelly markers. Or the bubbles.

"But Lisa, every time I bring the chalk/playdough/flubber/smelly markers/bubbles out, they go crazy!"

I'm going to tell you a secret. The reason they go crazy is because you never bring it out.

By keeping it in the cupboard and making yourself the keeper of the chalk/playdough/flubber/smelly markers/bubbles, you have elevated chalk/playdough/flubber/smelly markers/bubbles to the status of SPECIAL TREAT, and it will continue to remain new and novel, thus making the children "go crazy" each and every time you bring it out UNTIL the chalk/playdough/flubber/smelly markers/bubbles just become a part of what we do here. And that is not going to happen until the chalk/playdough/flubber/smelly markers/bubbles are available on Monday and Tuesday and Wednesday and Thursday and Friday. By having them available all the time (which doesn't mean they're always necessarily on display, it means we can access them), we are detoxing the kids off of thinking chalk/playdough/flubber/smelly markers/bubbles have a special-treat status. We are intentionally stripping the novelty away. After a few days, chalk/playdough/flubber/smelly markers/bubbles aren't going to be special or novel, they're just going to be chalk/playdough/flubber/smelly markers/bubbles. And now you can move on to more important things instead of being reduced to being the keeper of the chalk/playdough/flubber/smelly markers/bubbles.

There are times when the detoxing takes a mere two days and other times when it might take two weeks. This is why you stop and TAKE TEN! Ten days of doing nothing new except making observations, followed by your first baby step. And when you start your baby steps, you tackle them ONE AT A TIME. Seriously. I caution you not to minimize or downplay the importance of this. If having the chalk/playdough/flubber/smelly markers/bubbles available every day is your first baby step, then DO NOT do anything else new or different for a few days as everyone recalibrates to "chalk/playdough/flubber/smelly markers/bubbles being available" as the new normal. Buckling in and riding out the wave of newness until it reaches the shore is easier when you've made peace with your personal CONTROL issues. You might try to hold the wave back from reaching the shore, but you will be unsuccessful, so the chalk/playdough/flubber/smelly markers/bubbles continue to be a "special treat" and you are now caught in a never-ending, vicious cycle. That wave will keep rolling back through again and again until you get so frustrated and so overwhelmed that you just lock everything up in that cupboard!

So what does *riding it out* look like? Well of course it will look different for every class and every situation, but I can share one constant, one thing that WILL happen every time you go through this process: the Law of Thirds will come into play. What does this mean? After you TAKE TEN and identify your first baby step of change, one-third of the kids in the class are going to notice the change right away, another one-third will notice eventually, and one-third will never notice. And this is why you TAKE TEN in the first place! There is always a handful of kids (the first third) who immediately notice that you changed the rules of the game, which is why before doing anything new, you take time to mentally process and consider the potential ramifications of your baby step. You need to have conversations with colleagues. You need time to think it all through. Not to plan a response to every possible outcome (that's impossible), but to reflect on what the overarching responses might be when you start down the path of a being a facilitator within a space that has few restrictions and who is controlling the environment instead of the children. Where might this baby step of change lead us??

I had a parent tell me once that the reason they thought I was good at my job was because they said I provided (their words) "anticipatory care" for children. As in being one step ahead and knowing where something might go, so I am already ready to deal with whatever *that* might be. And since I don't have a dog in the fight (meaning I have no emotional investment or a preconceived notion or an agenda in the direction *that* takes), I am just prepared for whatever *that* might end up looking like.

Not to fall prey to sound bites, and shoot, we're probably approaching a time where some of you aren't even going to know who this guy is anymore, but back in the day a guy named Wayne Gretzky was considered the best hockey player in the world (Google it, young ones). Born in 1961 in Ontario, Canada, he holds the record for number of NHL goals to this day and continues to be considered "the great one." But this isn't a book of sport stats, so what's the point? When Gretzky was on the ice, he consistently anticipated where the puck was headed. When asked why he was the best hockey player, he replied that it was because his dad told him to skate where the puck was going, not where it had been. We can afford to take a page out of Gretzky's book. Taking the time to ask ourselves, "Where might this go?" is good advice for us as early childhood people.

To be a facilitator means that you are ready and willing to assist when called upon. An online search said to facilitate means *to bring about* or *to make easier*. I think the intention of the word *easy* in this context isn't one of "taking the easy way out" or of being lazy but more of being there to assist in the process—whatever it might be—that is unfolding. Being comfortable assisting in whatever is unfolding is drastically different than needing to be the boss of whatever is unfolding. To put it plainly, being a facilitator is going to be much more complicated for control freaks.

Let's use a few of the scenarios from the last chapter to elaborate on what it means to be a facilitator.

Scenario 1: The Shoe Bucket

Q: What should I expect? Where might *this* go? What should I anticipate?

A: Everyone is going to take their shoes off. Multiple times throughout the day. At group time. During snack. Inside and out. At times when you don't mind and at times when you do.

Q: Why?

A: It's something that "wasn't allowed" and now it is! That's exciting! "But wait a minute, is it really the new thing? I'm not sure, so I'll test it." Again and again and again. The children are wondering both out loud and internally, "Is this REALLY how it's going to be? I can take my shoes off whenever I want? Or is this some temporary idea she picked up at another workshop?"

Suggestion 1: This is why you TAKE TEN! Stay consistent with the new structure. Make sure you are not doing anything else "new" other than this. You will be asking yourself, where might this puck go? And because you ask this of yourself, you are already anticipating excited children and the need for (initial) constant reminders as to where removed shoes and socks go. You are already planning for providing extra time for putting shoes and socks back ON. This is riding out the wave—KNOWING that all these little variables are important *and* are going to require your time and attention as everyone recalibrates to this new "new."

Suggestion 2: Do a quick body scan: Are your teeth clenched? Is your jaw clamped shut? Shoulders tight and up by your ears? Are you holding your breath? Be mindful of the timbre and inflection of your voice as you provide reminders. Stay neutral. Be aware if you start to get frustrated. Children can smell your frustration because your body language will give you away.

Q: What else should I anticipate?

A: Possible pushback from administration, colleagues, and/or licensing who might insist/claim/say that this behavior is "not allowed."

Suggestion 1: Know your rules and regulations. If you are expected to be aligned with something, you should be familiar with its content.

Suggestion 2: Be ready to ask for proof of such claims so as to not have any one person's personal preferences dictating the direction you take in the classroom. Example: if someone says it's a licensing regulation, ask to see what page it is on.

Anticipated outcomes: (1) The kids who really need/want to be barefoot now have a consistent structure. (2) The ones who were just testing the new system know you were serious (it wasn't just a "good mood" thing) and know there's a structure for when/if they want to take their shoes off. (3) You have educated yourself on the actual rules and regulations and are not caving in to personal preferences.

Scenario 2: Standing Up at Circle

Q: What should I expect? Where might *this* go? What should I anticipate?

A: Everyone might stand up.

Q: Why?

A: Same as scenario 1. While you didn't necessarily make a grand announcement, per se, you changed the rules of the game when you responded differently than usual to the situation at hand. Again, this is exactly why we TAKE TEN! Not rushing into new behaviors allows you to ease into change! You have a head start because you have taken a few days to start processing the change, but you must remember that the children have not! It's new! It's different! Aaannnnd just like with the shoe bucket, they are going to test it!

Suggestion: Stay consistent with the new structure. Make sure you are not trying to implement any other new things!

Q: What else might happen?

A: The children, depending on their ages, might become more interested in having a dialogue about standing, sitting, who can see, who can't, and so on.

Suggestion 1: Realize that facilitating this dialogue is NOT an "interruption," and it is very much more important than getting to the end of the book.

Suggestion 2: Start becoming OK with putting the book down.

Anticipated outcomes: (1) Children who want to stand up realize it is not going to cause a power struggle. (2) Children who can't see realize there might be more than one way to solve their problem. (3) You begin to buy in to the fact that dialogue and communication really are more important than getting to the end of the book. (4) You start to believe that children standing up at circle is not going to jeopardize the credibility of your program.

Scenario 3: Eating Playdough

Q: What should I expect? Where might *this* go? What should I anticipate?

A: Everyone might, and I STRESS *might*, start eating the playdough.

Q: What do you mean by *might*?

A: I mean that this situation requires you to have TAKEN TEN! The minute you do the mom noise (GASP!), it's like opening a doorway of doom that all the kids are going to jump through, even if they HAD NO INTENTION OF EVER EATING THE DOUGH!

Suggestion 1: Simply just having a nonemotional, neutral response to the behavior (whatever it might be) and stating what the children *can* do, versus reinforcing what you *don't* want them to do, is frequently all it takes for them to change direction and/or stop the behavior because the children see that they are NOT getting a rise out of you.

Suggestion 2: Just like in the other scenarios, you are not going to make a grand announcement that the children are now allowed to eat the playdough (first off, that would be instigating, and second, sorry, would also be stupid), but if/when someone does eat it, you now respond calmly instead of overreacting.

Anticipated outcome: Unless we are dealing with pica (a persistent tendency to eat dirt, paint, ashes, and other nonfood substances that have no nutritional value) you can expect the behavior to stop on its own if you are consistent with neutral redirection and if you believe that it will stop. The minute you let your brain go off on a "Well Lisa, you don't know THIS kid!" tangent, the behavior will go on and on and on. The body follows the mind. Please remember that this specific scenario will often redirect itself if you are calm. For example, if you notice someone about to take a bite, a calmly stated verbal redirection such as, "You can _____ or _____ the dough" might be all that is required.

Scenario 4: Activity Time

Q: What should I expect? Where might *this* go? What should I anticipate?

A: No one is going to do your project.

Q: Why?

A: Not being forced to do the Teacher Planned Activity might be a new thing. The kids are going to be testing and wondering (just like in the other scenarios), "Is this REALLY how it's going to be? Or is it what will be allowed today, but not tomorrow??"

Suggestion: Stay consistent with the new structure. (Do you see a pattern emerging?) Make sure you are not doing anything else "new" other than having the Teacher Planned Activity now be a choice instead of mandatory.

Q: What else might happen?

A: The room might get a little louder than usual.

Q: And why is that?

A: Previously the children have been told when they can do stuff. Now they are getting the opportunity to choose on their own. They are going to be excited!

Anticipated outcomes: (1) Adults and children are no longer getting into power struggles over classroom activity choices. (2) Adults relax their perceived belief that everyone has to do everything at the same time. (3) Adults strengthen their ability to attach "learning words" to what might look like "just playing" to someone who walks in.

Reminder! All of these scenarios require you to have TAKEN TEN *and* be willing to RIDE THE WAVE OF CHANGE! Don't shut down just because the room got a little louder than normal, because everyone stood up, or because no one wanted to do the activity. Stick with it! I promise, once children see and trust that this *is* how it's going to be, they mellow out and everyone recalibrates to the new normal.

As a facilitator, my role is one of setting the stage (the environment) and then providing both time and opportunities for the children to deeply explore, investigate, ponder, and engage with the materials and people within that same space. The idea of being able to explore *deeply* is important but isn't possible with prepackaged curriculums that are a mile wide but an inch deep. Exploring *deeply* takes time, so when a hurry-up-and-stay-on-task mind-set rules the roost, fast-food curriculum becomes more convenient. And, like real fast food, it isn't sustaining or good for you. Scripted curriculum that come in the mail, in a box, from a corporation that is 1,500 miles away is not relevant or meaningful to the children in your program. The *things* in your space, things like ideas, activities, items, and materials, should be dictated by the ages, stages, ideas, and interests of the children who show up on a regular basis. As Katrina Gutleben cleverly states, "Learning can only happen when a child is interested. If he is not interested, it's like throwing marshmallows at his head and calling it eating."

When the activity dictated by today's lesson plan doesn't have any context for the children in the room but I feel I *have* to do it, there is a strong chance I am now *instigating* instead of *facilitating*. Instead of blindly going with the flow, I want you to start asking questions! Where did the expectation to teach children about X, Y, or Z come from? A mail-order, prepackaged, fast-food curriculum? My coteacher? Where? Whose idea was it? Mine? If so, why? Am I deepening something I observed organically from the children's play or conversations? Or do we always talk about birds the third week in March?

Back before I knew better, I would often put out baking soda, vinegar, and big soda bottles. You know the drill! Put some baking soda in the bottom of the bottle, pour some vinegar in, and BOOM! Watch the reaction! The kids say, "Again! Again!!" I still do this with children when I'm hanging out with them, with one subtle (yet huge) difference: I used to announce, "Today we are doing volcanos!" even though it isn't one; it's a chemical reaction. I realize this might sound like an issue of semantics, but if you think about it, most of you reading this don't really have real-time exposure to volcanos. So why would I *instigate* an investigation of something that the children can't really see, hear, touch, or smell? Now, if I put out the materials and we make a few explosions and then the children offer, "It's like a volcano!" that is entirely different from me instigating an investigation of volcanos even though we live in the middle of Oklahoma and we always do volcanos the third week of July! I am not going to shut down the child's comment. I'm going to use reflective listening (remember that?)—I'm going to repeat back what I heard them say and then take the time to see where it goes.

Does it spark a conversation? Does someone remember a trip to Hawaii? Did someone see something on the news? Was it a passing comment? I will wait to see what transpires before deciding what my next step might be because it might launch into a full-blown discussion and investigation or it might be an in-the-moment conversation that tapers and fizzles out on its own. Again, I am not going to jump to any conclusions! And I don't need to because I am a *facilitator* in a place that values the importance of *time* and of self-reflection, so I am not feeling pressure to hurry up and react to it. I have time on my side. Because of this, I can wait and see where this might organically go without having to fold, spindle, or mutilate it into some kind of a teachable moment.

For the sake of conversation, let's say this scenario evolved into something that even three, four days later, the kids were still talking about. Clearly this idea of a volcano is something that has captured their attention. Now, depending on where we are located, I might or might not have the ability to bring IT to them or THEM to it. Chances are, though, I don't. So what do I do? I need to be as (remember my phrase?) developmentally inappropriately appropriate as possible. What can I make as *real* as possible and what might have to be more *abstract*? What books does my library have? Do any families or coteachers have any resources we can tap into? What is the *thing* about a volcano that the children have locked on? Explosions? Heat? Lava? And how can I bring some representation of *that* into the room? Harnessing as much of the real as possible is totally different from transforming the room into some kind of clichéd Hawaiian theme with ideas I gathered from Pinterest.

When the environment is set up with materials that are relevant and meaningful to the children in the room, when teachers can link what's happening to the four domains of DAP, when adults know when to step in and when to step back, when adults engage in self-reflection, when children have enough time to explore, and when the adults know how to translate what children are doing into language that resonates with those who don't see playful learning connections on their own, we are doing our job. This is being a facilitator.

During workshops I like to ask how comfortable people are with the idea of children directing their own learning. Of course everyone thinks it's a GREAT idea until you have them define what it means and then share what they think it might look like. Maria Montessori is credited with saying, "The children are now working as if I did not exist," and I would say this should be a goal of sorts for all of us in early childhood. About six weeks into a new school year, you, in theory, should be able to leave the room (I know you won't, but you SHOULD be able to do this) without worrying that the room is going to collapse into some chaotic manifestation of exaggerated anarchy. If you look at me with that, "Well shoooot, I'm not sure . . ." face, I am going to gently inquire as to whether or not you drank the Kool-Aid of thinking you need to be in charge of everything because you are the *teacher*.

So on one hand, I will state that Bev Bos taught us that the adults in the room need to be less egocentric than the children, and on the other I will ask, did anyone talk with you about this before they threw you in a classroom? Did anyone ever talk with you about the importance of turning inward and considering how our egos would respond as we started being better facilitators? What issues DO come up? We must take the time to turn the mirror inward. Self-awareness is a big part of the process of becoming a facilitator (versus an instigator) because it is only after we take a good hard look at ourselves and our control issues that we can **release** our need to be the boss of everything. Only then can we remove the keys that open the cupboard from around our necks! Our continued need for control over children, or our gradual release of it, will determine how successful we will be when it comes to embracing a child-centered philosophy.

Someone said once that good teachers are more of a guide on the side than a sage on the stage. I agree. To paraphrase author Anna Quindlen, at some point we must move to the sidelines of children's lives, which is where we belong if we did our job right. Yet we aren't moving to the side because we aren't interested or because we aren't paying attention—oh no! Just the opposite. When I am comfortable being on the perimeter instead of always up in everybody's business, I, literally and figuratively, am able to make better observations. My observations allow me to see what children are truly interested in, what they might need to keep their investigations and explorations moving forward, and they allow me to consider what my role in the process might be. Yet a common challenge to engaging in active observation is that when we are observing we often don't feel like we are *doing* anything. We trip ourselves up and get all in our heads. We worry about what would happen if someone walked in. We ruminate over whether or not it looks like we are *teaching*. We start second-guessing the value of observing, wonder why we bothered getting that master's degree, and convince ourselves that everyone walking by the window thinks we must be lazy slack-offs.

Yet our observations assist us in making sure that we are offering rich, meaningful, relevant opportunities and experiences. But what is a rich, meaningful, relevant opportunity or experience? I'd say it is one that might be useful or have purpose. It could be practical or something that is important or of interest to the child. It could be something that has context to their life or maybe something to which the child feels closely connected. It may be a situation where direct instruction is appropriate or something entirely self-initiated. Regardless, it requires time, thought, observation, and relationships. All of which take more effort than mindlessly executing scripted fast-food curriculum, covering the walls with Pinterest-inspired craptivities, and stocking the shelves with battery-operated toys purchased in frantic haste the last day of a conference because they were on sale.

I have long viewed myself as a *facilitator*. What do I mean? I think it's my job to arrive at school before the children so I can prepare the room to be ready to receive them. The first fifteen minutes sets the tone for the rest of the day, and I want to start calm. Taking the time to prepare the space allows this to happen. I am not running around emptying the trash, cutting orange slices, and filling paint cups as twenty kids show up at the door. After preparing the space and getting the room ready to receive the children, my job is to pay attention, listen, notice, and use these observations to determine my next course of action. Does something (someone?) need to be redirected? Is someone exploring an area they have never been to before? What could have prompted that? I am making mental notes and taking real ones. Does someone need assistance with something? How do I know? Does a different child need a new challenge? Again, how did I know? Am I witness to play or conversations that might prompt me to make an intentional provocation tomorrow to see if that adds depth to an ongoing project?

As a facilitator within a child-centered environment, my job is to set the stage and then step aside while still paying attention, to be, as a child told me once, always in the middle but never in the way. Which can only happen when we reframe the lens through which we view the role we play in the classroom: as facilitators instead of the almighty *teacher*.

6

Adults Are Able to Articulate the Intention behind Their Words and Actions

EVER PLAYED buzzword bingo at a meeting? At a conference? During a professional development event? While on a conference call? All industries have their buzzwords, short phrases or words that serve as effective shortcuts when having conversations with people who are aware of the context. But a problem with these phrases is that they can quickly become overused clichés that have been drained dry of their original meaning. Of their *intention*. Which brings me to my point: the phrase *intentional teaching*. This implies teaching done with purpose, where actions and words are deliberate and we are conscious of what we are doing. Intentional teaching is a *crucial* component of a child-centered philosophy, so when it started looking like it was on the fast track to buzzword status, I began to worry. We cannot allow ourselves to shorthand the importance of genuine intentional teaching.

The Lisa Murphy definition of *being intentional* means being able to answer three questions:

1. WHAT am I doing?

2. WHY am I doing it?

3. WHO is it for?

ECE BINGO

Proficiency	Mindfulness	Outcomes	Rigor	Readiness
Grit	Developmentally Appropriate Practice	Differentiated Instruction	Meaningful Observation	Intrinsic Motivation
Peer Assessment	ST(t)(r)(r)E(a)(m)M	FREE SPACE	Brain Based	Early Literacy
Disposition	Scaffolding	Evidence Based	Multicultural	High Quality
Approaches to Learning	Growth Mind-set	Relationships	Core Competency	Deep Play

And let the record show that because you are now working diligently at setting up an environment where children can be engaged in any and all areas of the room, where outside time isn't hurried, rushed, and only taking place once a week, where you see yourself as a facilitator instead of being reduced to simply a rule-enforcing behavior cop, you have the *time* to start asking these questions.

WHAT? WHY? WHO? Keep track of your answers. And (now I'm going to up the ante) if at any point your honest answer is "I don't know," then you are NOT allowed to continue doing whatever it was until you do. Read that again. If you don't know why you are doing it, you aren't allowed to do it again Until You Do. STOP. Do not pass GO. Do not collect $200. Cease and desist.

Why? Because if you know what you are doing and why you are doing it and who it's for, you are being genuinely *intentional* in your practice.

Otherwise we could simply just be going through the motions, discon-nected from a WHAT or a WHY, perhaps just doing something because it has become a habit or routine. Maybe someone told us that's how it had to be done, so we signed on, signed up, and just got with the pro-gram without ever questioning anything. There's no need to drag this out—the simple yet challenging focus of this child-centered attribute is really thinking about things and then asking questions. This focus contains within it another rationale for my suggestion to TAKE TEN! Thinking about things can be exhausting. Shoot, simply starting *to be aware of the things we should be thinking about* can be exhausting! Let alone starting to ask questions!

And here's another thing, when you start asking yourself the WHAT, WHY, and WHO questions, I'm going to challenge you to demand a deeper answer from yourself than "because it is *cute*." As in, we do it because it's such a *cute* activity! It's so *cute* when they do that! We need to **break up** with thinking that CUTE is an acceptable rationale to con-tinue doing something.

Cute is a four-letter word that un-dermines the experience. Author Mary Renck Jalongo says that cute activi-ties insult a child's intellect, mistake doing with learning, often miseducate, undermine educational equity, and compromise professionalism. So the next time you find yourself doing something, planning something, purchasing something, or, dare I say, repinning something because it's cute, ask yourself, "Can I substitute the word *relevant*? Can I substitute the word *real*? How about *meaningful*?" And if not, circle back to the three orig-inal questions and begin again. What am I doing? Why am I doing it? And who is it for?

> ### Things to Break Up with Review List
>
> twenty-minute time blocks
>
> moving like a herd
>
> asking fake questions
>
> lifting children to equipment
>
> telling kids what we don't want them to do
>
> making moral issues out of developmental ones
>
> allowing CUTE to be a rationale for planning/doing/buying something

And here's another suggestion: remember to ask yourself the three questions before buying anything for your classroom or program. Who is this for? Who needs it? So often at those big conferences we get sucked into those final-hour sales pitches of 80 percent off and promises of FREE SHIPPING! We remember to ask, "How much is this?" or "What age group is this for?" or "Do you take Visa?" but rarely do we ask, "Who needs this?"

Why is this an important question? Because we *all* have been bamboozled in a vendor hall, spending more than half of our take-home pay for more stuff that, sure, we scored a great deal on, but we neglected to consider why we needed it and who we were purchasing it for. So we go back to school on Monday, exhausted from all the travel; the late-night, after-hours networking; and those godforsaken, crack-of-dawn, early-morning workshop sessions, armed with ten, fifty, maybe hundreds of dollars worth of puzzles, puppets, books, games, and whatnot only to realize (quite quickly, mind you) that no one really cares. And it's at this moment we feel the shift in ourselves—a shift from having a financial investment in what we brought back to school to having an emotional one. We start getting upset because—gosh darn it!—we bought all this stuff and NO ONE is using it. Now our egos get involved! We get a little agitated! Someone get over here and play with this! Do you know how much this cost? We nabbed a great deal on this for you guys! You don't know how lucky you are!

And while I applaud your willingness to purchase for your classroom and your ability to lock down a great deal, guess what? You forgot to ask *who needs this*! And that is why half of it will remain shoved in the back of the already overflowing storage closet with the crap from last year's conference that no one "appreciated," and the other half you'll find yourself dusting as it sits untouched on the classroom shelves.

Noah used to shove all of the flashlights into the pockets of his pants and run off to the bathroom because he liked to watch how the flashlight lights would bounce off the mirror when you turned off the lights in the bathroom. My child care licensing manager wasn't a fan of this. While you and I may see the *science* contained within playing with light, dark, reflections, and shadows, and the *language* of talking about his observations, she saw only a safety hazard (apparently there is an epidemic of children falling head-first in toilets and drowning that no one was aware of—note sarcasm) and thus pronounced that he was not to be allowed to do it again. Let me please say that I was far enough on my journey to not take her request as law, so I said we needed to find a compromise so he could play in the dark without her being overly (and unnecessarily) concerned. After some brainstorming, I came up with the idea to hang four sheets from the ceiling, clipping them closed with clothespins so as to create a vertical dark space, like a cave (can you see it in your imagination?), where he could bounce the lights off the sheets in a somewhat dark space.

And while anyone could go and play in it, who was it for? That's right, Noah. Which is entirely different from seeing an idea on Pinterest and being all like, "OMG that's so cuuuuuute!" and then you invest the whole weekend into making it happen. Your time. Your energy. Your money. The whole weekend was dedicated to breathing life into the cute! And it was all in vain because on Monday, what happens? No one goes in. Tuesday, no one goes in. By Wednesday you're like, "I was here all weekend making this for you! Someone get in there!" At which point you realize the cold hard truth, which is that you might've made it for yourself.

What are you doing? Why are you doing it? Who is it for?

Why IS it "bird week" the third week in March? Are the birds returning from their southern migration? Did someone make the connection between the chickens they saw during the field trip to the petting zoo and the lunch menu? Is there a new bird sound in the yard? Did one fly into the window and die? Did someone find a nest or eggs in the yard? Did someone get one for a pet? These are a few examples of relevant, real, and meaningful, not to mention developmentally appropriate, reasons to possibly consider investigating the topic of *birds*. "Doing birds" because that is what the Kute Korporate Kiddie Kurrikulum kit says you should be doing the third week in March, is not.

Who SAID you had to make a paper-plate fish for art today? Is it "F" week? Why? Why do they all have to do the same thing at the same time? Why are we interrupting rooms full of engaged children to make them come to the table? Why are there still expectations for thirty-minute mandatory circle times? Who said you can't move the easel outside? Why can't you have a classroom pet? Why do they have to sit crisscross applesauce? What if my EARS are on you but not my eyes? As early childhood educators, we find ourselves continuing to drink a lot of Kool-Aid even though it's leaving sour tastes in our mouths. It's time to put the cups down and question why we keep drinking! The shorthand phrase I use to identify the various things I'd encourage you to start questioning is *programmatical hams*. I want you to start questioning your programmatical hams. I'm going to tell you a story and then you will understand why that is what I call them:

❧ ❧

Once upon a time, there was a mom who was in the kitchen preparing a holiday ham. Her daughter was in the kitchen with her, watching her actions. Before putting the ham in the oven, the mom chopped both ends off of the ham, then put it in the pan. Again, her daughter was watching. "Why did you chop the ends off?" asked the daughter. "Well, that's what you do," said Mom, "that's how you bake a ham, you chop the ends off first." "Yes, but *why*?" asked her daughter.

Caught off guard, Mom realized she didn't really know *why*, that's just what you did (she thought to herself), that's what her mother had taught her. She was busy with holiday preparations and didn't really have time for this right now, so with a frustrated edge to her voice she said, "That's just how you do it, that's what Grandma taught me, you chop the ends off first." "Well whhhyyyy did Grandma do it?" asked the daughter. Having reached the end of her patience, Mom said, "Grandma's in the other room, go ask her!"

So the daughter went to the living room and found her grandma. "Grandma! Why did YOU chop the ends off the ham?" Much to her dismay, the daughter received the same response. "That's just what you do. You always chop the ends off the ham before you bake it." "But WHHYYYYYYYY?" asked the daughter, who was now beginning to feel frustrated herself. "*Why* did you chop the ends off?" "Well," said Grandma, "I really don't know. That's just what Great-Grandma taught me. Let's go ask her . . ."

So they got up and walked upstairs to where Great-Grandma was resting. "Great-Grandma!" asked the daughter, "Tell me please, why did YOU chop the ends off the ham?" *(You see what's coming don't you?)* "Well, I've never really thought about it," replied Great-Grandma. "I guess it's just what you do. It's what my mother did. You just always chop the ends off the ham before you bake it." The daughter whined in frustration, "Yes, but why why why?" "Well," said Great-Grandma, "I guess I don't really know, let's go ask Great-Great-Grandma."

So now daughter, Grandma, and Great-Grandma went down toward the porch where Great-Great-Grandma was sitting in the rocker with her knitting. The daughter burst through the screen door almost screaming, "Great-Great-Grandma! Please tell me! WHY DID YOU CUT THE ENDS OFF THE HAM?"

Great-Great-Grandma paused and, barely looking up from her knitting, said, "Gracious, child, my pan was too small." The End.

❀ ❀

Moral of the story? We now have multiple generations of ham cookers who think YOU MUST CHOP OFF THE ENDS OF THE HAM, but really they don't because their pans are plenty big! If you have heard me tell this story in a workshop, you know what I am going to tell you next. If not, stay with me and follow my train of thought. In your program, your practice, your teaching, there will more than likely always be a HAM you choose to chop the ends off of. Here is what I expect of you if you embrace a child-centered philosophy: *be able to tell me why you did it.*

All I ask of you from this point forward is that you make a commitment to be able to articulate clearly and confidently your WHY. We can have a philosophical debate another time. Whether you choose to *do* something (make product-oriented paper-plate craptivities for art) or *not* do something (don't allow the use of food or shaving cream in the in the sensory bin), I want you to be able to tell me *why.* CUE DRAMATIC MUSIC: I dream of a time when people in this profession are able to consistently articulate the intention behind their language, actions, and choices and also of a time when it's required for them to be able to do so.

But that's the way we've always done it is dangerous thinking. For ninety-nine different reasons. Many too tragic and way too off-topic to address here. But I think you get my drift. Someone told me once that "But that's how we do it here!" is the final battle cry of a dying organization. The programs we create for children need to be built on stronger rationales than dying battle cries. They deserve better from us and we deserve better from ourselves.

One of my "big things" is knowing why you are in the field in the first place. It takes work and effort, patience, dedication, and commitment. If you are in it for the sticky kisses, hugs, and finger painting, you are going to burn out pretty fast. Those things are pleasurable by-products of our job, sure, but they will not sustain you in the long run. Our job is hard. Holding yourself accountable to being more intentional in your practice is HARD. It requires conversations, which require trust and relationships. And that can be hard too. It demands a willingness to turn inward and engage in self-reflection. Which is also hard. It forces us to come face-to-face with all of our *shoulds* and our values and our expectations. Bev Bos and Dan Hodgins talk about the *spells* we are under as teachers. Spells such as no food (beans/rice) in the sensory tubs, no food for art (pudding paint), mandatory circle time attendance, shoes must stay ON at all times, "one-two-three, eyes on me," weekly themes . . . It is both challenging and GOOD to start unpacking our spells, but here's the catch: we must be able to reflect on these spells without engaging in any self-blame or judgement. Maybe we knew better, maybe we didn't. We may choose to remain under certain spells while breaking free of others (which can be EXTRA difficult if your coteacher wants to stay under a spell that you are ready to shed!!).

Breaking free can only happen when you are intentional in your practice, and that means asking yourself my three questions: WHAT are you doing? WHY are you doing it? And WHO is it for?

Scene 1

"I'm not allowed to use food"

"Why?"

"Not sure, I was just told that I can't."

"Go find out why . . ."

Scene 2

"We can't bring the easel outside."

"Why?"

"Not sure, I was just told that I can't."

"Go find out why . . ."

Scene 3

"I have to do small-group time every day."

"Why?"

"Not sure, I was just told it's required."

"Go find out why . . ."

This is what I mean by having the philosophical debate with you another time. We can get to that later. Demanding that beans and rice be allowed in the sensory tub (as an example) is not the hill I want to die on; making sure that people in this field are able to tell me why they are or are not putting beans and rice in the sensory table, IS.

THIS is intentional teaching. Being able to articulate the WHY behind our work. It's time to come out from hiding. For too long we've been allowed to take refuge behind the apron strings of supposed licensing regulations (that might or might not actually exist), off-the-wall demands of people who don't know any better, and our perceived expectations of colleagues and parents. We have given up our power and occasionally find ourselves teaching from a place of *fear* instead of intentional developmentally appropriate practice.

 BREATHE

Choosing to not do small-group time *and* being able to walk me through your thought process as to how you arrived at that point is drastically different than simply not doing it because you were tired, not prepared, hungover, didn't really want to, didn't really get around to it—the intention is vastly different.

Choosing to "get a two" in a specific category of a rating scale or evaluation tool because you are able to articulate why a certain material or medium is developmentally beneficial for children in your room is better than "getting a five" because someone told you anything less wasn't allowed and you never inquired why not.

A scary truth in our profession is that occasionally we find ourselves face-to-face with a realization that some of the Kool-Aid we've been drinking has gone bad. Subsequently, we find ourselves in a position of needing to make a change in our belief system or our practice. This is way more challenging than we realize. Remember what I said a while back about drifting. It happens. Drifting isn't the problem. Staying where we've drifted because it's become comfortable, is. Recalibrating is a time investment, but it's how we manage our growing pains. To get to the next level, we need to go through whatever THIS is. And to do that, we need to believe that what is on the other side (intentional teaching) is worth the time and the effort of constantly asking WHAT are we doing? WHY are we doing it? WHO is it for? Because it is only by asking these questions of ourselves and our program that we are able to avoid the steep, seductive, slippery slope of superficial, easy, and cute.

7

Adults Are Familiar with the Key Contributions of Historical Child Development Theorists

WHY?

Valid question. And without oversimplifying or undermining the work of classic and modern researchers, here's the long and short of it: nothing I have shared with you in this book is new. None of it. The theory that supports the creation of child-centered environments is solid and sound. The importance of long periods of free time to explore a rich, engaging environment with adults serving as facilitators, who are taking steps to control the space instead of the children, who believe in the inherent value of play and the significance of spending time in the outdoors, is not a new idea.

I am an advocate of child-centered, play-based, developmentally appropriate early childhood environments because they are what research tells us is best practice, NOT—say that again—NOT because it's *fun* or because it might appear to be my personal preference. It's not just what I *want* you to be doing; my ego isn't that needy! You might think it's a no-brainer, but it's worth repeating: *nothing* I'm putting out here for you is new. Everything I'm sharing here with you is grounded in research and in our profession's history. But here's the catch: we can't pull strength and credibility from the fact that it's not new if we aren't aware of who else said it!

Both newcomers and those of us who have been around awhile will benefit from knowing (or revisiting) the main contributions of the people who have historically paved the way. I'm talking about people such as Friedrich Froebel, Lev Vygotsky, Maria Montessori, Jean Piaget, Rudolf Steiner, Loris Malaguzzi, and John Dewey (to name a few). You can find volumes about each of these people individually and in collective works, or maybe you took a class that talked about them, or perhaps you attended a workshop like the one I did at The Association for the Study of Play (TASP) Conference in Albuquerque, New Mexico, called *Plato to Playdough*. (Clever, right?!) So whether you are familiar with these folks already or not, please allow what I am including here to serve as a *brief* snapshot into the lives of a few of the "masters" who have influenced what we do.

Friedrich Froebel

Froebel (1782–1852) lived in Germany. After his mother died, he went to live with his uncle (after his dad remarried), where he was free to roam the woods. During this early part of his life, he established a strong emotional connection to nature, gardens, and the outdoors in general. Although he started out as an architect and had a passion for the study of crystal formation, Froebel became a teacher after studying under Swiss educator Johann Pestalozzi, who, incidentally, believed that children learn by *doing*, who stressed the importance of hands-on manipulatives such as blocks, beans, and pebbles, and who stated that relationships were crucial. Froebel went on to develop what we call kindergarten (a literal translation of *children's garden*) at some point between 1837 and 1840. Some of his beliefs included hands-on learning being the best way for children to gather new information, that children need to be active, that direct observation is the best way to plan lessons for children, and that children need to be engaged in self-directed activities while the teacher is to serve as a guide. Froebel designed a series of playthings called *The Gifts*, which consisted of a systematic presentation to the children of various blocks, balls, cylinders, weaving, paper fold-ing, cubes, wooden tiles, sticks, rings, and architectural framework activities that provided, according to Froebel, educational experiences for his students. Up until this point, toys were seen as amusement while books and direct instruction served as the main methods of education. Although he was very strict in how The Gifts were to be used, his initial intention was to flip the existing mind-set and show that play could be the engine for learning while The Gifts served as the fuel. Froebel's goals for his students included the daily opportunity to engage in physical activity, to develop physical dexterity, to increase sensory awareness, to have outlets for creative self-expression, to sing, to have time for exploring ideas and concepts, and to have the experience of being with others, and overall satisfaction of the soul.

Maria Montessori

Montessori (1870–1952) lived in Italy. Although she started as an engineering student, Montessori went on to become the first woman to graduate from an Italian medical school and become a doctor. Her early work included working with children who were in asylums. She quickly noted that in many cases it wasn't the children who were sick or ill or had problems, it was their *environment*. At the request of the government, she left her medical practice and her university chair (in anthropology) to open a school called Casa dei Bambini to keep more than fifty children of working parents off the streets in the San Lorenzo section of Rome. It was here that she developed what we now call the Montessori Method. There were no materials for the children to use, so she invented them, and they are still used in Montessori classrooms to this day. One of her initial observations was that when the environment was prepared, was orderly, and provided experiences that were relevant and meaningful to the children, she didn't need to coerce them to show up—instead, they did so willingly. Controlling and establishing the environment is at the heart of her educational philosophy, as is making sure the environment is filled with opportunities to engage the senses, providing children with lots of time to explore, and providing real tools and materials for their use and investigation. She believed that teachers needed to set the stage and then step back and facilitate, that engaged children should not be interrupted, and that observation is at the core of effective teaching.

Lev Vygotsky

Vygotsky (1896–1934) lived in Russia and initially planned on teaching literature, but before graduating from the University of Moscow, he switched to law so he could practice beyond the limits set for Jewish teachers. Vygotsky is usually associated with cognitive and language development and is considered a cultural psychologist. Similar to Montessori, he felt that social conditions give rise to what we call "disorders." While conducting observations he noticed that within a group of children of the same age and developmental level, there were some who learned with little help and some who needed more assistance. Out of this observation came Vygotsky's idea of zone of proximal development (ZPD), which essentially means that **this** is what a child can do on his own, but **T H I S** is what he can do with assistance, and the assistance provided is referred to as *scaffolding*. One of the unique things about Vygotsky's work is his acknowledgment that children can provide peer-to-peer scaffolding; scaffolding is not just left up to the adults. He valued the interactions between both adults and children and felt that relationships and conversations were key to advancing knowledge. He felt that observation was at the heart of successful scaffolding and believed that children should be provided real tools and props in the classroom. Vygotsky believed that learning takes place when children play and that while at play children behave beyond their age as though they are "a head taller than themselves." Vygotsky died at a young age (he had tuberculosis) and was often lost in the shadow of Jean Piaget (more on him in a bit). Had he lived longer, Vygotsky's contributions to child development could have surpassed those of Piaget. The modern educational curriculum called *Tools of the Mind*, advanced by researchers Elena Bodrova and Deborah J. Leong, is profoundly influenced by Vygotsky and those who continued his research after his death.

Rudolf Steiner

Steiner (1861–1925) was an Austrian spiritualist and philosopher. He created the Waldorf system of education, which occurred after he gave a lecture to the employees of the German-based Waldorf-Astoria Cigarette Factory. After the lecture, the factory manager and Steiner collaborated to create a school for the children of the employees based on Steiner's ideas and teachings. This is why the system is referred to as *Waldorf* (after the factory) and not, as might be expected, his last name (Steiner). There is a strong belief in Waldorf schools that children learn by doing, as well as a huge emphasis on relationships and the importance of social skills; children often stay with the same group of peers for the duration of their education and in some instances, the same teacher stays with them too. Activities that might be considered frills in some programs, such as knitting, music, dancing, art, crafts, and gardening, are central to a Waldorf education, and electronic media is discouraged. There is a noticeable rhythm to the day in a Waldorf program, with order, beauty, and harmony being key characteristics in a classroom. Waldorf uses what is often referred to as an *upward spiral*, meaning the same basic knowledge continues to be introduced, but as the child matures, so does their understanding of the topic, thus allowing the topic to become more complex and integrated with each introduction. There is a strong emphasis on the whole child, and it is often said that a Waldorf school offers education of the heart, the hand, and the mind.

Loris Malaguzzi

Malaguzzi (1920–1994), like Montessori, was also Italian. Malaguzzi began his career as a teacher and went on to become the founder of Reggio Emilia's (a town in Northern Italy) educational philosophy. During his career, Malaguzzi oversaw both the birth and building of the region's wide network of infant, toddler, and preschool centers. His educational philosophy is frequently shorthanded to simply *Reggio*, but it is so much more than a philosophy or a curriculum: it is a way of life firmly rooted and intertwined with the community it grew out of, with family, school, and society fiercely interconnected. One doesn't "become Reggio" by removing clocks, hanging fabric from the ceiling, replacing plastic containers with baskets, installing wind chimes, or establishing an atelier. I say this not to be snarky, but in response to the fact that *Reggio* happens to be the educational bandwagon the US is currently riding, and there is legitimate concern that we are going to ride it to death due to an embarrassing lack of understanding of what it truly represents. But this, my friends, is a story for another day. A Reggio program values relationships, project work, emergent curriculum, and the arts. There is an emphasis on beauty and aesthetics and community collaborations. Teachers plan the day around the natural ebb and flow of interactions, activities, and the children, not a clock. Reggio values documentation (making the learning visible) and observation and places much of the learning in the hands of the students where the environment is seen as "the third teacher."

Jean Piaget

Piaget (1896–1980) was a Swiss psychologist who got started in child development after taking a job standardizing a French version of a British IQ test where he noticed a consistent pattern in the *wrong answers* being given by children of similar ages. This observation turned into a lifelong exploration of the question, "What thought process are they using?" The answers he gathered greatly influenced our early understanding of how children progress through stages of cognitive development. Piaget believed in the power of free play for children. He believed strongly in providing open-ended, real experiences for them and felt that children were capable of doing things for themselves. Piaget believed that play and curiosity were central to learning and that a teacher's job was to nurture inquiry. Piaget strongly disagreed with what we now call the *jug and mug theory*, and instead felt that teachers should be providing problem-solving challenges, not just dispensing (from their *jug*) facts and information (into the children's *mugs*). Piaget felt that curiosity and wonder were key ingredients to education and that it was impossible to *make* anyone learn anything. He believed that young children construct knowledge through what they do and what they experience, and Piaget served as a primary influence for what we now refer to as *constructivism*. Piaget's original beliefs have been at the heart of most nursery schools and preschools in the United States.

John Dewey

Dewey (1859–1952) was an American philosopher who led the progressive education movement in the United States. At the time, progressive education meant believing in anything different from the jug and mug theory that children should speak only when spoken to and learn through rote memorization and recitation. Dewey was considered a *radical* for proposing that education could be more self-directed, interactive, and child centered. Dewey felt that children learn by doing and need real experiences that encourage both experimentation and independent thinking. Central to Dewey's educational philosophy was that school and life were interrelated, and, as such, school needed to include a child's social world for it to be relevant. Dewey believed that curriculum needed to be based on a child's interests and a teacher's observations. For school to be meaningful, it needed to be more than just *fun*. Additionally, Dewey felt that teachers had the responsibility to be able to articulate the intention and purpose behind their actions and decisions.

 BREATHE

Do you see any patterns? Overlaps? Similarities? See the eclectic influence of these child development theorists in my work? I do a workshop where we go through these guys one by one, and the most common response at the end of the session is, "Well, look at that, they were all singing the same song!" Exactly! And just in case you plan on eventually giving yourself an independent research project, I'd currently add Magda Gerber, Emmi Pikler, Sara Smilansky, Abraham Maslow, Erik Erikson, David Elkind, Howard Gardner, Maxine Greene, Bev Bos, Lilian

Katz, and Vivian Paley to the list of names you should be familiar with. That being said (I'll own it), I believe you should have a working knowledge of the key players in your industry no matter what line of work you are in! I about died when I met a teacher at a Montessori school who didn't know there was a woman named Maria Montessori, when someone at a conference asked about Mr. Reggio (it's a town, not a person!), and when a group of kindergarten teachers didn't recognize the name Froebel, I was like, HE INVENTED WHAT YOU DO! How does this happen? I really don't want to come across as judgmental, but dang, how does it happen that you end up working in the field without ever learning about these guys?

What they *did* influences what we *do*. Knowing our history allows us to understand why we do some of the things we do. Take the idea of *observation*, for example. Let's say your director or college professor told you that *observing children is important*. Given the professional dynamic between you and your supervisor, you'd probably take the statement at face value and would therefore start *observing*. And honestly, there's nothing initially wrong with this . . . until you find yourself observing without really understanding why, or wondering what it is you're supposed to be looking at (or for) in the first place, or what you should be doing with what you are noticing. You find yourself asking, "Now what?"

Now compare that scenario with someone who was not only told that observation of children is necessary for creating developmentally appropriate environments for children but was also given a brief overview of the thoughts of some of theorists who agree with its importance (Vygotsky, Montessori, Piaget) and a list of some things that begin to happen as we gather observational data in the classroom (scaffolding, redirecting, documentation, lesson planning, developmental assessment).

The other positive thing that happens when we do our homework and learn about what these theorists added to the profession is that we **break up** with some (or all!) of the clichés and myths we may not realize we have subscribed to. For example, that Montessori is for rich kids; that Waldorf kids breast-feed until they're twelve, make their own paper, are pagans, and dance around the maypole every afternoon; or that getting rid of the plastic toys and adding pine cones and baskets makes you Reggio.

Here's the other thing: as much as it kind of makes me cringe at the truthfulness of it, never underestimate the potential power of a strategically placed name-drop. And this goes for the classic "masters" as well as our current modern researchers. What do I mean? Well if you have been in the field for any length of time, you have probably had your share of conversations with parents, coworkers, a boss, your administrator, maybe the owner of the program about how they want X to be happening in the room, but the expectation of X isn't really developmentally appropriate, so you go 'round and 'round about it. They are insisting that X happen, and you're making a sound, solid case for Y instead. Well, the honest truth is that in some situations, you can make point after (valid) point for Y until you are blue in the face, but there is just no convincing them. Until, instead of it sounding like Y is your personal *preference*, you say something like, "Well according the recent reevaluation of the pedagogical contributions of [insert someone's name here], the general consensus among modern theorists is that the expectation of Y overrides the more historical practice of X." Or "Based on a literature review of the ten most recent articles dealing with [topics], [Famous Name] has proposed that early childhood programs reconsider the expectation of X and make a plan for transitioning to the more developmentally appropriate expectation of Y."

But to do this successfully, ya gotta read the articles and you gotta know who wrote them.

Which brings me to another topic I'd like to toss out for your consideration: The Binder Challenge (TBC). Now I make a point of not recycling content from book to book to book, but I am going to make an exception in this case for a couple of reasons: (1) This might be the first book of mine you have read; (2) even if you read the outline of TBC that I included in the intro to my *Play* book, it is worth revisiting, especially if you have not yet accepted the challenge or if you skipped over the intro; and (3) if you have already accepted the challenge and started your binder, good for you! Take a beverage break and then come back for some affirmation.

For years I have been saying that I no longer feel it's on me to have to defend the importance of play. Why? Because that work has already been done. We have years of research, scores of articles, and issue after issue of journal after journal that have done, and continue to do, the heavy lifting for us. The current task facing developmentally appropriate early childhood educators is not *doing* the research, it is connecting both the naysayers and the supporters of a child-centered philosophy *to* the research. And you are not going to be able to do this if you are not familiar with what is out there! I am not saying you need to quit your job, go back to grad school, and obtain funding to conduct quantitative research on the value of *play* (although HUZZAH for you if you do!). What I am saying is that it is important for us to be familiar with the key contributions of various early childhood theorists! If we don't know what they said, if we haven't read the articles, if we are not familiar with the names of the current movers and shakers in the industry, our arguments for best practice are built upon nothing more than hashtags, slogans, and sentimental sound bites, and sadly, that is not enough.

As I previously mentioned, being child centered, play based, and developmentally appropriate is not a *preference*. We are not demanding play-based preschools because it's what we *want* or because it's what we *like*, but rather because that is what is supported in both historical and current research.

True story: I was on my way to a gig where I had to cross an international border and go through customs, then immigration. After the usual questions and inquiries (Where are you staying? What are you doing here? What do you mean by "early childhood educator"? Why so much luggage if you're only here for a short time? Why do YOU have to be the one doing the presentation?), I had been waiting for at least three hours (it happens) when the agent casually started talking about his two young children who went to a (his words) "Steiner school."

"Oh," I said, "a *Waldorf* school."

Without missing a beat, he stamped my passport, handed it back to me, and said, "Safe travels."

Was the agent testing me? Who knows. Maybe he was, maybe he wasn't. All I know is that in my brain, because I could make the connection between knowing that a man named Rudolf *Steiner* started what we call *Waldorf* schools, I was allowed to leave the immigration holding area. So there ya go.

Focus, Lisa! Focus! What does any of this have to do with a *binder*?

In a nutshell the Binder Challenge is simply this: First, get a binder. On the cover write:

PLAYFUL LEARNING = READINESS

PRESENTING THE EVIDENCE

Then, from this point forward, each and every time you find something that supports what we are talking about in this book, you are going to copy it and put it in your binder. It could be any or all of the following: an article, a letter to the editor, an op-ed piece, a photograph, highlights from a book you read, a book report, a book review, workshop notes or handouts, a blog post, website links, research studies, scholarly papers, undergrad- or grad-school-level papers or projects. *Anything* that supports playful, developmentally appropriate, child-centered, relationship-based early childhood programming now gets read, copied, and put in your binder so that when someone comes into your classroom or office and is all like, "It just looks like they are just playing all day here!" you can confidently say, "Playful learning is school readiness. This [point to the classroom] is what it looks like. And this [point to the binders] is what supports it."

As hard as it might be to not scream AND Y'ALL GOT SOME READING TO DO! I recommend self-restraint! Some will read what you've gathered, some will trust that you have done that for them, regardless, it reinforces that classroom and program choices are rooted in research, not personal preference. This gives credibility to our actions and assists us in our efforts of being more *intentional* (child-centered attribute six). Being able to support your "we stay outside for two hours every day" policy with a few reliable data points from the research of Joe Frost and his colleagues as to the developmental benefits of *playgrounds* (child-centered attribute two) goes above and beyond a rationale of "kids like being outside," which, although true, is limited and leaves you open to objection and pushback from folks who will make a counter-point similar to the "kids like candy too" argument.

Please know my intention here is not to make you think you need to read everything out there or memorize the names and dates of the historical early childhood "masters"—I am not giving you a homework assignment. What I am saying is that if there are things you believe strongly about when it comes to children and the environments they are growing up in, it behooves you to be familiar with a couple reasons WHY you believe those things that go a bit deeper than you just *thinking* or *feeling* that they are important. You don't need to write a thesis on the topic (although I will support you if you do!), but making the investment of putting time into locating a few articles that reinforce your position and a few names of like-minded wizards can make all the difference in the world when talking about your classroom or program; it will pay you back dividends. Your position is less likely to be poked, prodded, and constantly challenged when you are able to show that it's not just you. There really is strength in numbers. You have a team and a tribe; I suggest having a working knowledge of who they are. By embarking on an intentional investigative tour of our early childhood history and our theorists, we are able to discard clichés and stereotypes while bringing credibility and deeper knowledge to our teaching practice.

8

Adults Are Aware of the Importance of "Keeping It Real"

IF YOU'VE SEEN the movie *The Big Lebowski*, I'm sure you have visions of The Dude in your mind right now, "Keep it real, man." If you're *not* familiar with the film, shame on you. Just kidding. But it *is* a modern classic. Anyway, the kind of *real* I am talking about here is more of a literal one. Young children are not yet able to think abstractly. If you want something in their *heads*, it needs to first be in their *hands*.

Children need *time* to use all their senses to start making sense of the world. And they need real stuff. Adults in a child-centered environment celebrate where children are developmentally *right now,* and are not overly focused on where they *should* be, or where we *want* them to be. Being child centered means you are facilitating the exploration of real materials and objects, not coloring dittos of them.

If a child has the opportunity to eat, explore, cook, examine a *real* apple (child-centered attribute eight) and *time* (child-centered attribute one) and maybe she picked that apple off a *tree* she *climbed* by herself (attributes two, three, and four) in a real apple orchard (attribute two), and we were talking about apples because we live where apples grow, we have fruit trees in the yard, and it's harvest time, not because it was A-A-A (say it with me!) Apple Week (attribute six), not only does the exploration of an apple have context to her life, to her story, and her narrative but, thinking back to the four developmental domains of DAP—cognitive, language and literacy, social-emotional, and physical—when investigating a real apple, we are providing an opportunity to strengthen all four of them.

- counting the seeds = cognitive development

- picking out the seeds = physical development

- attaching various words to the experience of eating the apple, like *juicy*, *sour*, *sweet*, *sticker* = language and literacy development

- voting on their preferred kind of apple (red? yellow? green?) = cognitive development, language and literacy development

- working together to make applesauce = social-emotional development, cognitive development, physical development, language and literacy development

- cutting the apples = physical development

Shall I continue? The list of developmental goals being met will grow for as long as I want to dissect the activity. And you can conduct this dissection (so to speak) on everything you observe children doing in a classroom when it is being facilitated by caring adults who pay attention and who are well versed in DAP.

It breaks my heart that still, to this day, in too many classrooms A Is for Apple is for the first month of school; is for plastic apples to count; and flashcards for "reading" even though every kid named Alison, Andrew, Amanda, Alejandro, Annabelle, Ashton, Aaliyah, Aaron, Allie, Adam, Alice, Aiden, Amelia, Arthur, Abigail, Alfie, and Armando thinks, "That's MY name!" when the teacher holds up the card reading A-P-P-L-E! And don't forget the photocopied reproducible apple "work-shits" for coloring. With (your choice!) either a green or red crayon. Year after year after godforsaken year. Think back to child-centered attribute number seven and the importance of *intentional* teaching, WHAT are we doing? WHY are we doing it? WHO is it for? Remember what I told you Bev Bos used to say, you must be able to bring *it* to them, or *them* to it. And if you can't, you need to ask yourself how you expect children to be learning about something that isn't even in the room.

I can hear all the *but but buts* and am reminded of an article I wrote called "So Whattya Think about Themes?" The title is the same as the question I am often asked at workshops, and here is my standard answer: theme-based teaching isn't necessarily a bad thing; the way it's often executed is. Filter this title of the article through what we've discussed throughout the previous chapters and I am sure you will come up with the answer. What is the actual theme? Where did it come from? Whose idea was it? Is it relevant? Real? Meaningful? Cute? Does it have context to the children individually? Collectively? Is it developmentally appropriate? Are the children able to direct some of their own learning when it comes to this theme? Or am I the keeper of the stuff? Can I bring IT to them? THEM to it? What are we doing? Why are we doing it? Who is it for?

Let's walk through the most common theme that gets questioned: *Dinosaurs*. First off, where did it come from that *dinosaurs* is what we are talking about this week? Do we always "do" dinosaurs the third week of October? Or did a few kids go to a natural history museum over the holiday and come back all gaga over the exhibit they saw? And even when that is the case, are they showing me this is a topic they want to explore more in depth? If so, how did I come to that conclusion? Or is it more of a one-hit-wonder kind of experience that might influence their dramatic play or outside chase play for a couple of days? The intentional gathering of observational data will assist in making the call as to whether this becomes a topic for further investigation or not. And if it does morph into something we explore further, how am I making it as developmentally appropriate as possible? How do I present the experience without taking it over? How can I turn as much of it as possible over to the children? How do I practice sitting in the role of facilitator versus instigator? How might we add *depth* to the exploration versus just tossing out plastic dinosaur animals and reading a few books? And how comfortable am I in waiting for the children's language and play to direct what that *depth* might look like and the direction that might go?

This is exhausting work. My brain starts to hurt just *writing* about that process. But that is our job. The process of creating environments that are relevant and meaningful to children is sometimes way more *cerebral* than we realize. A willingness to engage in this kind of thought process is crucial if you are committing to a child-centered philosophy. And it takes *time*.

I invite you to filter what you are calling "projects" and "art" through this line of questioning too. If it is fish week, what do you need to have in the room? That's right, FISH. If for some reason you are not able to have fish in the room, and there's no place to go to see some fish, I need you to think about WHY you are talking about fish in the first place. Because that paper plate you cut up into the "shape" of one isn't teaching anyone about fish. And you know as well as I do that although the child might've painted the paper plate during "art," it was you who cut out the triangle fin and stapled it on at naptime.

If you want it in their heads, it needs to be in their hands, and if you want it in their hands, it needs to be in their hearts, and it won't be in their hearts if it's not something that is of interest in the first place. Not to sound like a brat, but I am not sure why we continue to overthink this. As adults we don't like having stuff done to us. We check out mentally if we aren't interested or engaged, so why do we get so surprised when two-, three-, and four-year-olds show us in very developmentally appropriate ways that they are not interested in the subject at hand? Why do we keep throwing marshmallows at their heads?

Some of our circle time rituals are easy targets for keeping the WHAT WHY WHO conversation going. Let's be honest, drawn-out discussions about the calendar and the weather aren't engaging to anyone. Do you know anyone who has discussions about today being W-W-W-Wednesday and tomorrow being TH-TH-TH-Thursday with anyone? Tamar Jacobson, author of *Don't Get So Upset* and *Everyone Needs Attention*, reminds us that adults only talk about the weather when they are bored at cocktail parties and have nothing else to say. As adults we freely admit that this is not real conversation, it is last resort, mindless chit-chat, yet we demand children to be still! and sit up straight! for long periods of time on a regular basis to engage in the same ridiculous banter! When I asked Tamar to share a comment with me for the book about some of these silly questions we ask children at circle time, she told me that whenever she hears a teacher ask children whether it's sunny or raining, she always hopes one of the children says, "Go to the window and look for yourself!"

Story break! As many of you know, I spent a good part of my teaching career in San Diego, California. One December we had a storyteller from Minnesota come visit us. While she was with us she proceeded to tell a group of preschoolers a very lively twenty-minute tale about *blizzards*. She went on and on about the snow coming down from the sky during a blizzard, how cold it is during a blizzard, how you have to shovel your car out because of a blizzard, how sometimes have to stay home during a blizzard; she went on endlessly about blizzards this and blizzards that. Now, to her credit she was a talented storyteller, so the children were totally engaged with her story; however, when she was done, one of my boys stood up and proudly announced, "Yeah, and sometimes blizzards are small and green and run really fast!"

I about died! She didn't get it. She looked at me and asked, "What is he talking about?" Seriously??!! No offense, lady, but what have *you* been talking about? These kids are from San Diego, they have *no idea* what you are talking about, so they are going to attach something that they do know about to this blizzard thing you keep mentioning. They had no idea what a *blizzard* was, but it sounds a lot like *lizard* and we had those everywhere!!!!

I accidently started a fight on an early childhood social media page when someone asked for developmentally appropriate ways to talk with children about the weather. When I replied, "Go outside," you would've thought I'd thrown a grenade into a pile of puppies based on the crazy responses my comment generated: "They need to listen!" "Children need to pay attention!" "It's important for them to learn about the weather!" "Be respectful!" "Next year they won't be able to go outside!" And so on and so on. But it doesn't make any sense! You do NOT learn about the weather by talking about it, you learn about it by experiencing it.

As adults, we would not tolerate someone grabbing us by the arm and telling us to sit back down and pay attention to a conversation so boring and benign, yet it happens to our young children on a regular basis. And we wonder why they don't like school. It's really not rocket science. I think one of the spells our educational system is still under is one of thinking school better not be of interest, because interest might lead to joy. And good gracious! We sure don't want anyone enjoying themselves here. Too many lesson plans and curriculum packets work from an outdated and inaccurate viewpoint that children see learning is a chore. Yet if you hang out with children long enough, you see that they are filled with unlimited supplies of curiosity and inquiry. For too many children, it is the environment (and all that unfortunately might accompany said environment: people, expectations, experiences, control, and so on) that squishes this fire out. John Dewey said that the problem with traditional schools is not in the absence of experiences, but in the fact that the wrong ones are provided.

"Right" ones are developmentally appropriate, they are real, they are relevant, and they have context to children's lives. It is only after having years of interacting with the *real* that children can successfully make the leap to understanding the more abstract. It's not that we think the abstract is too hard or we don't want to challenge them, it's that we are familiar with the existing research (attribute seven) about how children learn. We are able to articulate (attribute six) clearly and confidently that if you want children to eventually be able to X (think abstractly) loads of time (attribute one) with Y (the real, attribute eight) has to happen first.

Gluing cotton balls to construction paper is not teaching children from Texas or Arizona about *snow*. Nor is it teaching any child anywhere about *clouds*. Coffee filters are not snowflakes. Brown paint is not mud. Fish and watermelons are not made out of paper plates. A brown paper bag, painted orange, stuffed with newspaper, isn't a pumpkin. What are we doing? Why are we doing it? Who is it for?

Some programs expect children to start learning about the *seasons*. Depending on where you live, this could have context and be a springboard to authentic investigations of what is happening outside the front door, or can be downright hilarious. I've heard answers to questions like, "What season it is?" range from heated discussions about local sports (football season, hockey season, basketball season) to the contents of someone's spice cabinet (cinnamon, oregano, basil)—one child wondered aloud if salt and pepper counted as seasons, and I cringed as he was "brought back on topic,"—to conversations about the local hunting schedule (trout season, deer season, boar season), with occasional deliberations as to the pros and cons of gun or bow season all the way to a grand pronouncement made by a four-year-old who said his mother's favorite season was FOUR. At first I didn't get it, did you?

I found out later she frequently brunched at the *Four Seasons* Hotel in Carlsbad, California.

All of this is deep, meaningful, relevant dialogue! All of these (perceived) "off-topic" discussions are more relevant and *real* than trudging through some clichéd, canned curriculum about winter, spring, summer, and fall, especially if you live in an area that doesn't have a change of weather seasons. I've recently been spending time in Florida where I have learned there are two seasons, Summer I and Summer II, with Summer II occasionally including a subseason called roof repair. In Minnesota the seasons are Winter I and Winter II and the subseason is referred to as road repair, and guess what? They're *all* are right answers.

When we continue to put the cart (inappropriate expectations) before the horse (being developmentally appropriate), we find ourselves having to push and push, then, when children don't understand what we are stuffing down their throats, we push harder when what we need to do is back off and reexamine our intentions (attribute six) and make sure our expectations are developmentally appropriate and based on accurate early childhood research (attribute seven). And if you give a mouse a cookie . . . thinking about all of this is reminding me how literal children are and that makes me think about the theorists we talked about in the last chapter and that makes me think we might need to pause for a second and talk a little bit more about Piaget.

 BREATHE

In college I was basically taught that Piaget was the be-all end-all rock star of child development theory, one reason being that our country was still riding (although it was almost at the tail end) a developmental wave (versus academic) when it came to early childhood education *and* because the department chair studied under him. The program was very Piagetian. So it took me by surprise (and maybe some of you too) when the scientific credibility of his work started being questioned.

Now, while I am willing to acknowledge that yes, his sample sizes were too small, and yes, he should've provided more details as to how he selected his subjects, and yes, stage theories have perhaps fallen out of favor with modern developmental researchers, and yes, I'd agree that extrapolating data gathered from observing three children to *childhood as a whole* probably is pushing the envelope research-wise, I am not ready to throw the baby out with the bathwater. I would argue that Piaget still has historical significance, that his contributions to child development theory remain important, and that some of his findings (whether currently considered *valid* or not) remain constant, predictable, and true.

Like what? There comes a point when babies realize mom is actually *gone*. There is a day when an infant bends over the side of the high chair to look down on the floor because they know the rattle is *still there*. There are still toddlers who believe the moon comes out because *they* are going to bed. Young preschoolers who've not yet mastered conservation continue to think that a line of five same-sized blocks S P R E A D out contains more blocks than a line of five of the same-sized blocks SQUISHED together. And there will forever be preschoolers who, when you ask them, "What day is today?" will confidently answer MOVIE DAY! or PIZZA DAY! or THE DAY MY DADDY PICKS ME UP! not only because those facts are true, but because those things are more relevant and meaningful than W-W-W-Wednesday.

Piaget identified this "literal" phase as a stage of cognitive development he called *preoperational thought*. Their *literal* answers to our (sometimes poorly phrased) questions are not intended to make us crazy, they are contextual answers that give insight to their lives, their narratives, and their relationships. And these answers, while potentially frustrating, are so much more meaningful than children just shouting out MONDAY! for no reason other than the teacher lady said it's the *right* answer.

There continues to be a huge disconnect between what children really can do and understand and the curricular expectations placed upon them. Someone might tell you that children preparing for kindergarten should know the alphabet, so in response to this expectation, you sing the ABC song. A lot. But here's the deal, just because you know the song doesn't mean you know the alphabet. Everyone knows the song. But if you walk up to anyone on the street and ask, "What comes after K?" or "What comes before P?" Do you know what they do? They sing the song! Maybe not out loud, but definitely in their heads! Why? *Because no one knows the alphabet.* We know a song. Is there anything wrong with singing it with children? NOT AT ALL. Unless you think that by being able to sing it, the children now *know* the alphabet.

I observed a child being given an assessment of sorts where he was asked to circle the letter *N*—which he did, and then, without looking up from the paper, he asked, "Where is the other one?" I was intrigued. Not only by his question, but to see how the assessor handled it. All she said was, "Where do you think it should be?" and he put his finger right in the middle of the letters Y and Z. Confused? I was too. Until I sang the song. Do it. Sing the song out loud. If you are from the United States you probably do not enunciate the word *and* very clearly when you reach the end of the song "T U V W X Y *and* Z," so when you sing the song, it sounds like you are adding an N when you sing, "W X Y *'n'* Z."

Here's another one: I watched as a pre-K teacher painstakingly sang the ABC song with her students and then started in with the flash-cards. She held up the *A* card and asked the group, "What sound does this letter make?" A little guy said, "Shhhh, let's listen." Was he being a brat? Defiant? Does he need an assessment? NO! He's four! Same thing with the days of the week song. If someone somewhere is telling you that singing this earworm of a song is a noncompromisable and you MUST do it each day, then you know what, fine! Sing it! Then get on with your day. Don't hang out here and drill and kill children to death over whether or not they can recite the days. The only thing kids care about on a calendar is their birthday. Our profession is long overdue in making peace with this. The concepts of yesterday, today, and tomorrow are toooooo abstract for young children. Shoot! They wake up from nap and often think it's a new day!

Circle back to child-centered attribute number one, *time*. Remember it's not just about children having enough *time* to explore the space, but it's also taking the *time* to ask children real questions. Many of our (perceived) conversation challenges with children are due to the fact that we are not taking the time to think about what is about to come out of our mouths. When we ask hasty questions or make general statements we will receive very literal answers that make us say, "Whaaaaa??" (P.S. All of these are true stories.)

✦ ✦

David! Your shoes are on the wrong feet
    These are the only feet I got!

Scene: I was flying to Florida, we were taking off, the mama in front of me gave her young son a piece of gum, and all she said was, "Here, baby, it's for your ears." What do you think he did?

A three-year-old was shopping with his mom at holiday time. Tensions were high, and a lot was being packed into one day. The youngster announced, I HAVE TO POOP! Mom said, "Pinch your cheeks, you'll be fine!"

Scene: a room full of kindergartners are walking aimlessly around the classroom holding chairs. Some of them are crying. Principal asks the frustrated teacher (who was a sub from the fifth grade classroom, mind you) "What in heaven's name is going on here?" Teacher says, "Honestly I just don't know! I just keep asking them to take their seats!"

Child asks, "What color is this crayon, Teacher?"
    "Oooh, that one is hot pink!"
    Child dropped it to the table and started blowing on it.

There was a new child in first grade, the teacher asked her, "How high can you count?

The new student dragged a chair over to the table, put it on top of the table. Climbed onto the table, *then up onto the chair* where she began to count "1, 2, 3, 4 . . ."

I asked my nephew to put catsup on the table. He was three at the time. And yes, he squirted little piles all over the table.

Child started his first week in kindergarten. His mom, also a teacher, wanted to ask engaging questions of him when he came home: "What did you talk about at lunch?" she asked. "Nothing" was his reply. Day after day, all he said was, "Nothing." Finally, she asked why he didn't talk about anything at lunch and he said, "Because the lunch lady said we're only allowed to talk to our neighbor, and Jim doesn't go to my school."

A toddler teacher was wrestling with the children in her class, she got overheated and tired, so she left the wrestling mat saying (to the air), "Whew! I am pooped!" One of her young charges followed her off the mat, pulled the elastic on her pants, and "checked her" to see if she needed a diaper change! Upon seeing that she didn't, he announced in a confused, questioning voice, "You're not poopy?!!"

And the pièce de résistance: A pre-K teacher was working in a church-related program. During the Lent and Easter season, the priest asked the four- and five-year-olds what they knew about the Resurrection. One of her students stood up and said, "I know if it lasts longer than four hours you need to call a doctor."

And there you have it folks. You honestly can't make this stuff up. I offer these anecdotes not only for some comic relief, but to remind everyone reading that *this* is where children are developmentally. Putting the expectation cart before the developmental horse is not preparing anyone for anything and can often lead to high levels of stress and frustration for everyone involved. If individuals without any knowledge of child development theory continue establishing the curricular requirements for early childhood programs, AND THOSE WITH THIS KNOWLEDGE REFUSE TO PUSH BACK, there will be an ongoing (and expanding!) disconnect between expectation and ability. If we claim that our end goal is "readiness" for elementary school (and what does that really mean anyway?), children need to spend the years before that transition engaged with real, relevant, meaningful experiences like the ones we are going to talk about in the next section.

9

Children Are Provided Time and Opportunity to Create, Move, Sing, Discuss, Observe, Read, and Play (a.k.a. the Seven Things) Each and Every Day

MANY YEARS AGO I started presenting a workshop called "The Importance of Early Experiences" where I identified seven things we need to be doing with children every day and *why*. It quickly became one of my most requested sessions. Shortly thereafter, I received many requests for the material to be developed into a book, so I initially wrote *PLAY: The Foundation that Supports the House of Higher Learning*. Quite a few years later, after collaborating with my current publisher, Redleaf Press, we decided it was time to revise the *Play* book, so we gave it a new name, a new cover, and after an in-depth editorial facelift, voilà! we now have *Lisa Murphy on Play*. But many of you already know this, so what's the point? The point is that philosophical attribute number nine, the stuff I want to talk about in this section, already exists as its own workshop and as its own book! And this gave me pause while writing. Obviously I am not going to repackage the *Play* book. Instead, I would like to highlight the main points within each of the seven things, link them a little tighter to DAP, and wrap it up by exploring the Play Types as identified by Bob Hughes. My thought is that if you *haven't* read the *Play* book, this chapter will whet your appetite to do so, and if you have, you will get a few reminders as well as some new content. Sound like a plan?

Good.

Here we go:

So far I have presented eight attributes of being child centered that will guide us, philosophically, as we frame the foundation that supports the house of higher learning. In that house are all the academic expectations we place on children: knowing their name, letters, shapes, numbers, and so on. Attribute number nine, this chapter, is the foundation itself—making sure children have daily opportunities to create, move, sing, discuss, observe, read, and play. Please remember that play is not a separate, seventh thing. Play exists within creating, moving, singing, discussing, observing, and reading, serving as the metaphorical cement that is holding our foundation together.

Moving forward, let's establish that "early childhood setting" means a program, either in or out of a home, where children have daily opportunities to interact with materials that could be classified under the following categories: art, blocks, books/library, dress-up, math/manipulatives, science, playground/recess, writing/journaling, sand/water/sensory table, and playdough.

At a quick glance, in what areas are you likely to see children **creating**? Art, blocks, books/library, dress-up, playground/recess, writing/journaling, sand/water/sensory table, and playdough. Where are you likely to see children **moving**? Blocks, dress-up, playground/recess. How about **singing**? Books/library, dress-up, playground/recess. Where might they be seen **discussing**? Art, blocks, books/library, dress-up, math/manipulatives, science, playground/recess, writing/journaling, sand/water/sensory table, and playdough. **Observing**? Art, blocks, books/library, dress-up, math/manipulatives, science, playground/recess, writing/journaling, sand/water/sensory table, and playdough. Where might you see children **reading**? Books/library, writing/journaling, playground/recess. Where will you see children **playing**? TRICK QUESTION! It's

ALL play! Which is why we can say that play is the foundation that supports the house of higher learning! And while *I* know this and *you* know this, you will occasionally have to interact with folks who still think that when children play, they aren't learning, and learning better not look like anyone is enjoying themselves. Remember, this is what is called a *false dichotomy*, implying that you have to choose between one or the other. That somehow it is either play OR learning, when we know it's really a blend of both. But as usual, I'm getting ahead of myself. Let's break our foundation down into bite-size bits:

Making Time Each Day to Create

It should go without saying, but it's *the process not the product* when it comes to children's art projects. If the activity takes you longer to prepare than it takes the kids to do, it is probably product oriented. First, figure out where the need to do this kind of stuff came from, and then **let it go!** If you display children's art on the walls, adults should come in, tilt their heads in confusion, and whisper to you, "What IS that?" If they come in and ask, "Which penguin is Romel's?" and you have to look at the back of them all to figure it out because they all look EXACTLY ALIKE, it is probably product art. And while we're at it, why are you talking about penguins anyway? (And honestly, if you don't "get" the penguin comment I just made, I love you AND you are *required* to go back and reread child-centered attribute six regarding intentional teaching RIGHT NOW.)

While children should have daily open-ended opportunities to paint, draw, glue, cut, tape, and color, creativity shouldn't be limited to just the art center. Nor should children be forced or *made* to do art projects. Storytelling, block building, dress-up, putting together a puzzle, cooking, dancing, constructing a fort, using clay or playdough, and playing with Legos are just a few more examples of being creative. When programs embrace a broader definition of creativity, it becomes easier to link creating (as a part of the foundation) to the four domains of DAP. Which, depending on who you are talking to, can assist in making a stronger case for ensuring that children receive daily opportunities for creative expression.

Unfortunately, daily opportunities for children to express their creativity are still impeded by pressure (real or perceived) to do some kind of "project" (often a cookie-cutter, teacher-directed craptivity) for the children to take home, proving they did something at school. Creative endeavors that are more process oriented do not always manifest into some kind of tangible *thing* to bring home. There isn't always proof *per se* of what took place. How comfortable are you with that? How comfortable is your program? If your program is more process oriented, how do parents know this? What do you do if you receive a little pushback?

Inappropriate academic expectations often push creativity out of the picture. When ill-informed policy makers, directors, or curriculum writers expect young children to be able identify letters and write their names, we have an(other) example of putting the cart before the horse. And if we drink the Kool-Aid they are selling, we might find ourselves starting to think that we don't have time for finger painting anymore because we have to get children ready for school. Demands for young children to learn to read/write/compute are often seen as more important, so glue/scissors/paint get pushed out of the picture in the name of readiness. To paraphrase the Bard, *"Aye, but here's the rub!"* Children need lots and lots of time using their hands and fingers before they can be expected to write. And to have fingers strong enough to manipulate a pencil, children need strong hands, strong wrists, and strong upper arms. Big leads to little. Large motor leads to small motor. Gross to fine. Want kids with strong hands so they can write? They need to have had the opportunity to climb things. To run, jump, pull, and swing. Which isn't going to happen when recess is taken away due to readiness policies or litigation concerns. No one is saying that children shouldn't learn to write; this is just a reminder that they aren't going write just because the district bought pencils.

Additionally, did you know that young children will demonstrate about eighty different stages of scribbling *before* they are ready to write? Eighty! And even then, when young children do initially write their names, they don't necessarily "know" what they are doing. (Think back to singing the ABCs, it's the same thing, they can do it, but don't necessarily *know* what they are doing.) Initial attempts at writing are nothing more than a child putting a bunch of shapes together that, in turn, get a positive and enthusiastic response from an adult. There's nothing wrong with this—just realize the difference. When young children appear to be making letters, we need to remember that, to them, they are *shapes*, symbols if you will, not letters in the way we see letters. Which is why they will often start flipping and reversing and inverting them because they don't know (yet) the hard and fast "rule" that print is not flexible. To them, those "letters" are still shapes, so it doesn't matter how (or where) they are placed on the paper, because a shape is a shape is a shape no matter how it is rotated. Which doesn't mean we don't want them to learn how to write; we just realize it's not time yet. A child's development is better served by being engaged in more creative activities, not being at a table in a chair that's too big, with a piece of lined paper and a pencil they can barely hold "practicing their letters." Squirt-bottle painting, shaking a parachute, building with blocks and Legos, and squeezing a fresh batch of playdough are much better (read: developmentally appropriate) examples of fine-motor and prewriting skill development. Not to mention of creativity.

And now (say this in your best announcer voice!) get ready foooor-rrrrr . . . homework time!!! It's time to play LINK IT TO DAP! Read through the following creative scenarios and darken the circle of the developmental domain(s) being strengthened while the child is engaged in that activity. (Yes, I am asking you to write in the book. Again!)

When children write a letter to someone, using inventive spelling and drawing a picture to go with it

○ Physical   ○ Language & literacy   ○ Social-emotional   ○ Cognitive

When children make a PLEASE DON'T TOUCH sign for their block tower

○ Physical   ○ Language & literacy   ○ Social-emotional   ○ Cognitive

When children ask for their names to be placed on their papers

○ Physical   ○ Language & literacy   ○ Social-emotional   ○ Cognitive

When children work together to make a new batch of playdough

○ Physical   ○ Language & literacy   ○ Social-emotional   ○ Cognitive

When children grasp paintbrushes and any other material that might be used for painting, such as plungers, sponges, stampers, potato mashers, or fly swatters

○ Physical   ○ Language & literacy   ○ Social-emotional   ○ Cognitive

When children squeeze glue bottles

○ Physical   ○ Language & literacy   ○ Social-emotional   ○ Cognitive

When children move their arms to make huge brushstrokes onto mural paper

○ Physical   ○ Language & literacy   ○ Social-emotional   ○ Cognitive

When children use scissors to cut paper, playdough, or string

○ Physical   ○ Language & literacy   ○ Social-emotional   ○ Cognitive

When children manipulate dress-up props, such as zippers, snaps, laces, buttons, and belts

○ Physical   ○ Language & literacy   ○ Social-emotional   ○ Cognitive

When children use any kind of construction or building materials, such as recycled boxes, blocks, Legos, Magna-Tiles, Duplos, K'NEX, Kapla blocks, or Tree Blocks

○ Physical   ○ Language & literacy   ○ Social-emotional   ○ Cognitive

When children design train layouts, ramps, and pathways or marble runs

○ Physical   ○ Language & literacy   ○ Social-emotional   ○ Cognitive

When children assemble a puzzle

○ Physical   ○ Language & literacy   ○ Social-emotional   ○ Cognitive

When children announce that they need more paint

○ Physical   ○ Language & literacy   ○ Social-emotional   ○ Cognitive

When children use clay and playdough

○ Physical   ○ Language & literacy   ○ Social-emotional   ○ Cognitive

When children arrange small objects onto cardboard for collage art

○ Physical   ○ Language & literacy   ○ Social-emotional   ○ Cognitive

When children are spinning and twirling while dancing

○ Physical   ○ Language & literacy   ○ Social-emotional   ○ Cognitive

When children make up new words to a familiar song

○ Physical   ○ Language & literacy   ○ Social-emotional   ○ Cognitive

When children are negotiating who will be who in a dramatic play scenario

○ Physical   ○ Language & literacy   ○ Social-emotional   ○ Cognitive

When children move loose parts or furniture to make the scene for a play or to act out a story

○ Physical   ○ Language & literacy   ○ Social-emotional   ○ Cognitive

There's lots of learning going on when children are creating! We need to make room for all the different ways children express their creativity, not just the ones that go home.

Making Time Each Day to Move

Children grow from the neck down and the trunk out. Learning goes from the hands to the head, not the other way around. This is where we got the saying that if you want it in their heads, it needs to first be in their hands. Children need opportunity to move on a daily basis, and not just running around, large-motor, outdoor play kind of movement (that's a given, isn't it?) but inside too. Some children just simply need to stand up all day. That's OK. Someone needs to dump the Magna-Tiles out onto the floor before building with them. Someone needs a dance party before sitting down for a story. Someone will appear to always run and never ever walk. Someone will always say hello with their whole body. That's OK too. We must take steps to make sure that the adults in the room realize that young bodies are almost always in motion, whether they are inside or out! And while this doesn't mean we are throwing chairs and jumping off the tables in the name of a child's need to move, it does mean that adults have age-appropriate movement expectations of the children in the room and, equally important, age-appropriate *responses* to active behaviors that occur in the classroom too.

Diane Trister Dodge said that sitting still and being quiet is not a marketable job skill. We've already unpacked the importance of being outside (attribute two) as well as started the process of working through some of our responses when children do move around and stand up (attributes three, four, and five), so I have no intention of repeating all of that here for the sole purpose of jacking up the word count. What I need you to be able to do is articulate why moving is important and to have a rationale that goes beyond it being a fun way for kids to let off some steam while you get a little bit of a break. Why? Because there is a direct link between *moving* and successfully meeting some of the expectations we currently have of children.

A couple of examples: You can't be expected to hold a pencil if your hands aren't strong. You can't be expected to sit upright at a table or not fall out of your desk if you have never had opportunities to develop balance and coordination. And while it's not my place to get on a "the importance of a healthy lifestyle" soapbox, you don't have to be a gym rat or a professional athlete to know how much harder it is to get into the habit of becoming more physically active as an adult if you don't have any muscle memories to go in and wake up.

Now, as much as I know how much you loved the LINK IT TO DAP exercise I gave you a few pages back, you are smart people. I am not going to ask you to fill in what is being developed when children are engaged in large-motor activities. There's a whole damn domain devoted to the importance of large- and small-motor physical development, which means that no one really should be arguing with you as to the importance of activities such as playing with the parachute, running around the yard, jumping off a straw bale, hopping through tires, swinging, skipping, squeezing playdough, pulling a rope, dragging a log, carrying (or rolling) a tree stump from one end of the yard to another, galloping, crawling, playing tag or dodgeball, dancing, rolling down a hill, twirling, climbing a tree or over boulders, bike riding, playing hopscotch, riding a scooter, ice- or roller-skating, maneuvering through an obstacle course, going up or down a slide, digging with shovels, using hammers/drills/saws, building with blocks, or playing any number of various ball games.

Obviously, all the activities I just listed can be linked to the physical development domain of DAP. Which is why I want you to take it deeper. I want you to take a step beyond the obvious and consider how the same activities connect to the other domains. Want extra credit? Link the activities to other domains *and* identify anything the child might be "learning" while engaged in them. I am going to walk you through this challenge using *playing with a parachute* as the example. Then I want you to grab a colleague (or not) and work your way through a couple yourself. I know you are busy. I know you have other things requiring your attention, but we aren't going to get better at this until we start practicing. Deal? Deal. Here we go:

Also, and this is something I maybe should've covered a little more in depth a while back, please know that it is totally acceptable if an activity doesn't meet ALL FOUR domains within DAP. Don't stretch it. Don't make it fit all four if it doesn't. Does that make sense? Can you make a strong case as to how Activity X links to one of the four? Maybe two? Awesome. Start there. Build your confidence and practice verbalizing the obvious connections and links before hunting for the smaller, subtler, and maybe-not-so-obvious ones. Remember: they are obvious to you because this is your area of expertise and training. What might be a no-brainer to us might be a huge AHA to someone else!

What is the activity? A group of twelve mixed-aged (four-, five-, and six-year-old) children are playing with a parachute on the grass on the school playground.

State your initial rationale for this activity: When a child is [verbing the noun] *shaking the parachute* they are [translate the play that's happening into words the Person Who Doesn't Get It will understand] increasing both fine- and large-motor skills that are necessary for meeting future writing goals. How? Answering "How?" could sound like this:

> Shaking the parachute increases upper arm strength, which leads to wrist strength, which leads to finger and hand strength, which leads to the ability to hold a pencil. And grasping the edge of the parachute specifically assists in prewriting development by strengthening children's fingers so they can hold a pencil.

Not too hard, was it?

Let's keep going. Additionally, most parachute games have some form of descriptive/directional elements to them where children have to follow movement-oriented directions, such as some children being told to *run under* and *through* to the other side, or some children *walking around* the outside of the parachute, first in one direction and then in the other, while others *hold it up* in the air, or some children *crawl across the top* of the parachute while others *sit and shake* it. Not only is this more evidence of parachute play being linked to developing the physical domain of DAP but we are starting to spill over into language and literacy as well.

Let's stay here for a second. We'd be silly to think children aren't talking to each other and to the teacher while they are using the parachute, so we have the further development of language via basic conversation (this is also social) and literacy since children might be being exposed to new words (such as *grasp, shake, perimeter, clockwise, reverse*) while engaged in parachute play.

Want more? Parachute play also increases social-emotional development. SOCIAL in that children will have to interact with others while engaged in parachute games. EMOTIONAL in that they might have to deal with emotions related to (a) not getting a turn, (b) not being positioned next to a best friend, (c) getting "out" (if it's that kind of a game), (d) accidentally getting bonked by someone while moving under the parachute from one side to the other, (e) getting frustrated because their little hands keep dropping the edge of the parachute, or (f) the need to self-regulate when they might want to shake the parachute super super fast but right now they need to hold it up high so kids can run under it and over to the other side. (Or all of the above!)

We're on a roll! In mere minutes we have successfully shown how a simple playground activity (playing with a parachute) connects back to three of the four domains within DAP. We have one left. How *does* this activity link to cognitive development? At first it might not seem obvious, except maybe some basic counting skills (more formally referred to as *number sense*): "Kirin and Matthew left, we have room for *two more* kids over here!" Honestly, while this might appear to be a pretty

PRO TIP: Always be able to answer the "How?" question, but remember that a 101-level answer MIGHT BE ALL YOU NEED! Don't panic and assume you must provide some crazy, elaborate 501-level response to the question of "How?"

basic 101-level response, it is still correct and probably would suffice. If you want to step it up a notch though, you can do that too. With a little bit of prep, you can confidently state that playing with a parachute assists in developing early math skills! How?

- counting the number of children playing = number sense

- realizing that two kids have left and we need two more = number sense

- counting ten handles on the edge of the parachute = number sense

- realizing we need ten kids for each of the ten handles = representation (think one-to-one correspondence)

- ten kids playing means we need ten beanbags for shaking when we play the parachute "popcorn" game = representation

- going *under* the parachute = spatial sense (think shape, size, and position)

- understanding they need to *come out the other side* after running *through* = spatial sense

- lying down head to toe to see "how many kids big" the parachute is across = measurement

- announcing that the parachute is *big* but *light* = measurement

- announcing that it is a huge circle = measurement AND spatial sense

- considering how high the parachute is in the air when they hold it up over their heads = estimation AND measurement

- guessing how many kids might fit around the parachute = estimation AND number sense

- noticing the parachute's design is a repetition of the colors red, yellow, blue = patterns

- figuring out how to avoid the hole in the middle of the parachute when shaking balls and beanbags = problem solving

Your turn. Pick one or two from the following list, flesh it out a little and create a scenario, then link it back to the other domains of DAP: running, jumping off a straw bale, hopping through tires, swinging, skipping, squeezing playdough, pulling a rope, dragging a log, carrying (or rolling) a tree stump from one end of the yard to the other, galloping, crawling, playing tag or dodgeball, dancing, rolling down a hill, twirling, climbing a tree or over boulders, bike riding, playing hopscotch, riding a scooter, ice- or roller-skating, maneuvering through an obstacle course, going up or down a slide, digging with shovels, using hammers/drills/ saws, building with blocks, playing any number of various ball games.

This kind of work might seem tiring and tedious, but let me tell you, the time invested in getting good at this will pay you back tenfold! In a short amount of time we made a *very* strong case for the developmental value of a simple activity that, to the untrained eye, might seem like a silly playground game that isn't as important as something more *academic*. Yet by doing a little bit of homework, we are able to show that it *is* academic. Parachute play, like many of the other examples I listed, has the potential to strengthen each and every one of the developmental domains. Yet another example as to how playing is school readiness.

Making Time Each Day to Sing

Thankfully, it seems as though most preschools still make room for singing simply for the sake of singing, so let's run with that, shall we?! In order to take advantage of the fact that singing is still OK without needing to link it to an empirical, peer-reviewed study, the first thing we need to do is get over whatever kind of "I don't sing so well" nonsense we each might have in our heads. Then we need to start singing. Every day. To the air, to the kids, to the dog, to yourself. Bev Bos taught us that songs are the hooks to hang memories on. Want to know how therapists are making progress with clients with dementia and Alzheimer's? Music and song. Music has the power to rekindle connections where previously we thought there were none. Your very first connection to music was through your mother's heartbeat when you were still in utero. And the very last thing you are going to remember with word-for-word accuracy are the songs you learned when you were little. Songs and music have the power to influence you throughout your entire lifespan.

Music and songs can be very demographically specific, so I don't want to imply that the ones I know (or grew up with) are the ones you need to know. Don't overthink this. Just sing. And read poetry. What? Yes, poetry. And books with rhythm, pattern, rhyme, and repetition. This is not only language and literacy development but also cognitive development.

*I do not like them on a **train***

*I do not like them in the **rain***

*I do not like them, Sam-I-**am***

*I do not like green eggs and **ham***

Making time each day to sing also means being sensitive to the child who "doesn't listen" when you talk to him but is quick to "pay attention" when you start speaking in a singsong voice. If you discover that you need to sing to a child, do it. And stop right now with the "But no one is going to sing to her next year" nonsense. That's a bunch of *hogwash* (I had to say *hogwash*, I wanted to say something else but I'm well aware of the fact that I consistently push the "appropriate language" envelope). Get back on track, Lisa. Whether someone will or won't sing to her next year, right now it is NOT next year. It's right now. So if Daniella needs me to sing "get your boots and get your hat and get your jacket, we are going outside," why wouldn't I?

What songs did you sing growing up? What songs do you still know? What songs do you sing with the children? They will remember them forever.

When you sing, you are assisting children in the development of their language and literacy skills. Certain songs like "Willoughby Wallaby Woo," "Apples and Bananas," and "BINGO" also assist in cognitive development *in addition to* language and literacy. Good morning songs and other songs that specifically use the names of the children assist in social-emotional development. Fingerplays and any song that requires the kids to move around adds to physical development. Songs where children clap out the syllables of words is language and literacy, physical, and cognitive development. And songs that have verbal patterns, repetition, and require memory or recall develop both language and literacy and cognitive skills.

Singing isn't just a way to pass the time! There is a lot going on behind the scenes when you sing with children! Slow down a little and enjoy it. This isn't something to get through so you can move on to the important stuff, this *is* the important stuff!

Making Time Each Day to Discuss

While I would be hard-pressed to have to identify which of the seven things might be the most important, I will say that DISCUSS can be the hardest one to defend while in conversation with folks who "don't get it." Why is that? For the simple reason that discussing = communication = problem solving = social skills, and unfortunately, in too many circles, these skills are still seen as "soft" skills and therefore not as important as, say, counting or spelling your name. Which is interesting because while there is a huge social-emotional component to discussion, at its core is language and literacy. Which is one of the things everyone says we should be focusing on. Maybe at some point while we weren't paying attention, someone decided that talking about *some* things (The plot of a book? A math problem? The main points of a history lesson? Summarizing the results of a science experiment?) were more important than talking about *other* things (Feelings? Conflict? Frustrations?).

Here we are again! Face-to-face with the Bard's famous rub in that positive social-emotional development lays the groundwork for cognitive and academic competence. If you (claim to) desire a strong X, you must make room for developing a strong Y. Just as children learn from the whole to the part, they develop the same way too. Our attempts to fragment their learning continue to be in vain, how naïve we are to think we can conduct a math lesson and not pay heed to the *social* (I'm new here and don't know anyone), *emotional* (I like my new shoes), *physical* (but they're too tight), and *language* (I'm from another region and you talk really fast) variables of said math lesson. We continue to think that we can somehow arrive at a place of having a strong X by jumping over/ignoring/pooh-poohing the Y. When will we finally see that we can't have one without the other?

I am well aware that those of you reading this book are just as occasionally frustrated as I am. My ongoing intention, while multilayered, is pretty constant and consistent: First, to provide affirmation. You are NOT crazy or off base in thinking that there are times our society has lost its mind in regard to the demands it places on its youngest children. Second, research to assist us in our efforts of pushing back exists. Third, we each have a responsibility to be able to link the naysayers to said evidence. You can agree with me all day long, but if, at the end of the day, your only ACTION has been to express frustration, it's time to step up your game. Hanging out in your classroom with your nose in your phone while ooblick is dripping down the walls and you saying that the *kids had a great time* is not going to cut the mustard. If *kids learn through play* is your only ammunition, you are going to lose the battle and the war.

In my *Play* book I unpack in detail the importance of children learning how to talk with each other and the value of what I call "learning how to get your shovel back"—which in summary, is a loving reminder that it really doesn't matter if you know all your shapes and colors and can count to one thousand in six languages if you do not know how to get your shovel back from the kid who took it. This is still 100 percent true. Today I am going to add that it is just as important for the adults who work with children to be able to do the same thing.

How can we be expected to assist children in language development if we hurry through spontaneous, real-time conversations because we think staying on topic is more important?

How can we be developing literacy skills if the books we read are boring and patronizing, and have no real connections to a child's life or interests?

How can we claim to be modeling problem-solving skills if we hide behind memos and policies instead of having conversations and facing interpersonal, employee, or administrative issues firsthand?

How are we teaching conflict resolution if we have hard-and-fast "only three children at this center at a time" rules, which deny children the opportunity to figure things out? Or when we always interfere due to misplaced attempts at "keeping the peace," thus depriving children of the opportunity to practice the art of negotiation and compromise?

How is a child going to learn how to manage emotions when adults constantly bend over backward in noble but misguided efforts of keeping everything *fair*?

How will a child learn stick-with-it-ness (persistence) and resilience if all challenges are seen as hazards and safety threats and must therefore be avoided at all costs?

What is really being taught when adults insist that "we are all friends here"?

For too many years we have been drinking the "language and literacy and cognitive development are more important than physical and social-emotional development" Kool-Aid. It's time to dump out our glass and break the pitcher that poured it in the first place. Clarification: it's not that physical and social-emotional development are more important than the others; it's that they've been so grossly neglected for the last twenty or so years that the system is out of balance. All four developmental domains are equally weighted. But we won't be able to right the scale until *everyone* believes this to be true.

Over the years what kinds of conversations and discussions have you observed in your classroom? Are developmental skills (other than the obvious language and literacy) being strengthened when children have time to talk with each other?

I'll start. Let's consider the block area. What kind of language and conversations might we expect to see? Negotiation, sharing, making requests, cooperating, problem solving, describing the size/shape/texture of materials, directional language, counting, naming of shapes?

Seven children are in the block area. Four of them are working side by side (social-emotional, physical) and the other three are working independently. The four collaborators are discussing (language and literacy) how tall (cognitive) the building should be and the shapes (cognitive) of the blocks they want to use across the top. One of the solo players figured out how to balance almost twenty blocks (cognitive, physical) on top of a small yet sturdy foundational block. The other solo players are impressed and come over to ask about it (social-emotional, language and literacy). One inquires as to whether she will "help him make one too?" (social-emotional, language and literacy) while the other goes to the table and brings a chair over so they can "make it higher!" (physical, cognitive). One of the four collaborators accidently bumps (physical) into the initial structure and knocks it down. It falls over with a crash. One child appears upset (social-emotional) but is comforted by another player who says, "We can build it again!" (social-emotional, language and literacy) and they start to rebuild (physical). Two of the collaborators begin arguing over who gets to place the longest block (cognitive, language and literacy, physical) across the bottom until another player says, "You both can hold one end and do it together" (social-emotional, language and literacy, physical).

Your turn.

What other kind of conversations happen in your classroom? Which domains are being developed and what are children *learning* when they have them?

Making Time Each Day to Observe

The importance of observing means *intentionally* making sure children have time each day to use all their senses, not just during My Five Senses Week. Which we love, right?! It's so easy! Monday, touch! Tuesday, taste! Wednesday, smell! Thursday, see! Friday, hear! Yay! We did it!! All humor aside, please be careful not to reduce this to a checklist! Please take the time to consider how often and how authentically (meaning, it happens organically versus something you *planned*) children get to use all of their senses. What kinds of activities are the children doing on a regular basis that require them to use their senses? And can we link any of those activities back to DAP?

When you think about some of the many things children are able to TOUCH at your program: rocks, sand, paint, fabric, blocks, clay, puzzles, each other, ooblick, carpet, dirt, grass, mud, water, playdough, pets—each and every one of these has the potential to link to *all four* of the domains within DAP.

For kicks and giggles, let's use CHILDREN INVESTIGATING ROCKS as an example.

Noticing how the rocks are both similar and different in size, shape, and texture is both language and literacy and cognitive. Talking about how the rocks feel is physical and language and literacy. Learning from an adult or peer that this kind of round is also called *oval* and this kind of sharp can also be called *jagged* is social-emotional, language and literacy, physical, and cognitive (that's all four, guys). Picking the rock up in the first place is physical. Throwing the rock is physical. Helping the person it hit is social-emotional and language and literacy (and maybe physical, too, if you assisted in applying the bandage). Figuring out how to stack all the rocks on top of each other is cognitive and physical, and when you're so excited that you tell someone about it is both social-emotional *and* language and literacy. When you get so mad because your rock stack falls over that you yell out loud, that's also language and literacy and social-emotional, and when you get yourself reorganized and figure out how to make the stack of rocks NOT fall over, now it's cognitive, social-emotional, and physical, and when you ask for assistance to make a sign that says "Don't Touch!" it's also physical and language and literacy.

And that's just *touching* the rocks!

What about the sense of *smell*? Maybe not so much in this example. How about *taste*? Only that one kid. What about *seeing*? Yes! Now we're on to something! Children use their eyes to look at the rocks they've found, perhaps making observations about them and using visually oriented language to give directions about where to go to locate more rocks ("Over by the big tree"). They use their eyes to search for more, maybe using observations they've made visually to notice patterns in color, size, and shape (cognitive). They might be discussing the kinds of rocks they've found and their characteristics (language and literacy), and someone is going to want to make a chart or a sign of sorts (language and literacy and cognitive). And finally, what about *hearing*? If you bang two rocks together or throw one to knock down a pile, there will be a noise to hear. When someone drops one on their foot, there will be definitely be something to hear, probably some language too, and when others assist in helping, that's social-emotional.

When we have more fuel for our fires (read: language that increases the credibility of playful learning), the next time someone tells us that *rocks are not for playing with*, we will have a well-thought-out rebuttal that allows us to stand strong instead of backing down with our tails between our legs, head lowered, with our only response being a meek, "OK."

THAT is how things are going to change.

Providing opportunities for children to TASTE can be tricky with allergies and various food-usage policies, but what *are* you able to do? Sharing food increases community and relationships, which is social-emotional development. There is typically conversation around food, which is language and literacy. We might have a tasting party and then vote on our favorite fruits, that would be language and literacy and cognitive development. And using tools to peel, chop, and cut food is physical development too.

The sense of SMELL is utilized pretty often in a preschool setting! Remember that smell is linked to memory, and the smells children come into frequent contact with at the program are going to trigger memories as they get older. So what are their memories of this place going to be? Coffee? Freshly baked muffins? Paint? Glue? Or Pine-Sol and Simple Green? In general, the sense of smell links most strongly to language and literacy development because it's likely that children will want to identify a smell coming through the window from outside, or perhaps describe how their lunch smells. But on closer examination, even a common early childhood activity such as working together to make a batch of scented playdough is an opportunity to develop cognitive (all the math and science related to cooking), social-emotional (waiting for a turn to stir, being patient as the dough cooks), language and literacy (describing what they are doing, following a recipe, following verbal directions from the teacher, using vocabulary to describe the playdough), *and* physical development (using cooking tools, spoons, mixers, kneading the dough).

When children use their sense of SIGHT, they are also developing language and literacy skills as chances are they will want to talk about and describe many of the things they see. Looking at things might often lead to the asking of questions (which is language and literacy), the having of a big idea, or needing clarification about something, so we have the potential for cognitive development. Doing puzzles, reading, playing board games all use the sense of sight, and all of those are opportunities for physical, social-emotional, language and literacy, and cognitive development too.

Like with the senses of taste, sight, and smell, the sense of HEARING also has a strong connection with language and literacy development, and for the same reasons, children like talking about things they observe. Music activities could lead to physical development (dancing and marching), and games like Listening Lotto are opportunities for cognitive development. Being patient and listening while waiting for a turn during show-and-tell is social-emotional skill development too.

I think it's safe to say that daily opportunities for children to use their senses facilitates development in all the domains within DAP!

Making Time Each Day to Read

If you want kids to read, read to them! Do Not Overthink This. We continue to make more problems for ourselves and our profession when we think that what's already been proven somehow isn't enough! *When did we lose faith in what we know?*

There is a collective understanding that exposure to books, stories, and rhymes assists children in both cognitive and language and literacy development. This doesn't mean we make printable flashcards of the *Brown Bear, Brown Bear* characters or connect-the-dot workshits with Little Bo-Peep on them. It means we read to them. Storybooks, poetry, fiction, fables, tall tales, folktales, fairy tales, nursery rhymes, classic children's stories, the occasional how-to manual (don't laugh, it'll happen). Once in a while, the random stringed instrument from the seventeenth century is a big hit for some reason, so be ready, and don't forget about the ongoing, every-five-year request (it's like a flood cycle) for the history of railway transport (which means nothing more than procuring a big ol' picture book about *trains*).

It's been a few pages, let me tell you a story.

About fifteen years ago I did a presentation for my smallest group ever (and for those of you who keep track of this stuff, it's still the record holder of "smallest gig ever"). I was asked by a family child care colleague to do an evening talk for her families. "Sure thing!" I said. At the time I was also doing family child care, so I called it an early day (I had a great assistant, so I could do that) and drove a couple hours out to her program. Seven adults showed up. We were all in her living room. And for what it's worth, I did a very very young (still evolving) presentation of the seven things I am talking about with you right now. Anyway, after it was over and most of the other parents had left, one of the moms came up to me and said, very directly, coffee in hand, head tilted to the side, "I don't read to my daughter."

I was a caught a bit off guard, but not wanting to appear judgmental, all I said was, "No?"

"Nope, don't do it."

She appeared willing to engage, so I kept going. "Why not?"

"Because no one read to me."

"Is that so." I said it more like a statement than a question and then, attempting to gauge her response, I added, "Is that really why you don't read to her?"

"Really," she said.

And then, in one of those I-don't-know-where-it-came-from-but-it-was-amazing-and-I-don't-know-if-it-will-ever-happen-again-and-I-might-be-making-a-big-mistake-but-we'll-see-moments, I said to her, "Sit down."

She did.

I picked up the copy of *Brown Bear, Brown Bear* that I had brought with me, and I read it to her. Then I read her *Goodnight Moon* and then I read *Where The Wild Things Are*. And when I was done, I looked at her with (I'll be honest) a mix of confusion, disdain, sarcasm, and love and said, "*I* read to you. No more excuses. Go home and start reading to your daughter."

I don't know if she did or not, but what I *can* tell you is that twenty minutes a day and a library card will open the door to language, literacy, adventure, drama, imagination, and so much more. And there is so much evidence (not to mention common sense) about the importance of reading that I am not going to insult you or the profession in having you link READING to DAP. Language and literacy is its own developmental domain for crying out loud! If you run into anyone who thinks that reading to children is a waste of time, first, resist the urge to smack them upside the head and second, have them call me.

In the meantime, YOU keep reading. Preferably books that get children excited, engage them, have context in their world. Books that get kids talking on the very first page are the best kinds of books! Avoid books that are teachy and preachy. Practice reading out loud until you do it well. We tend to read to children too fast because we know how it ends, so practice *s l o w i n g* down a little when you read. Play with the intonation of your voice. Avoid books that are linked to TV shows or movies and other forms of commercialization. Books are going to occasionally get ripped, no worries, it happens. Get a big roll of clear packing tape and mend them. If some books are ripped and torn beyond repair, throw them in the trash (or the recycle bin) and get new copies. If you think the book is stooopid, it probably is. If YOU wouldn't want to sit through someone reading it to you, ask yourself why you are reading it to the children!

For those of you ready to level up, I'm including a step-by-step guide on how to do a book audit.

How to Do a Book Audit: Step by Step

First: No books related to movies, shows, or toys. This means no Paw Patrol, no Sesame Street, no Disney, no Barbie, no Bob the Builder, no Peppa Pig, no Sponge Bob, no Phineas and Ferb, no Garfield, no Thomas the Train, no Pokémon—you get my point. If you are really ready for an amazing book center, get rid of all the teachy-preachy ones, too, about brushing your teeth, washing hands, and how "we are all friends here." These get removed immediately for trash or recycling. Sometimes this process brings up questions about books that were books before they were movies: Clifford, Curious George, Madeline, and all the hijacked fairy tales (for example, I think *The Snow Queen* by Hans Christian Andersen is acceptable but *Elsa Goes Shopping* is not.) This can be tricky. How old are the kids? Did they know it as a book first? Or has the story always been related to a product or franchise for them? Is there a way for us to know? My rule of thumb is that if the book came out just as another product to sell the movie or show, it's out. If it existed before the movie, it stays in the YES pile and gets run through the rest of the criteria here to see if it passes muster. Especially point number six.

Second: No "push the button to hear the sound" books. These also get removed immediately for trash or recycling. Studies have shown that adults become overly focused on pushing the buttons the "right way" and asking closed, testing-type questions such as "Which animal makes that sound?" instead of enjoying the act of reading with the child. Consequently, the story and interactive banter that naturally occurs when reading a book-book gets lost.

Third: After you have cleaned out and removed the above, you must remove all the books you have never read and put them in another pile. We will come back to them in a minute. At this juncture you should have three piles: (1) trash/recycle, (2) books you *need* to read, and (3) books you are familiar with and have read.

Fourth: Next we will deal with that third pile: books you *have* read and you are familiar with. Go through each one looking for rips and tears. All books that are missing covers, missing pages, falling apart or are torn up beyond repair get added to the trash/recycle pile. No exceptions! I don't care how much it cost or how much they love it, it's MISSING PAGES! If they love it that much, go get another copy!!! Books needing minimal repairs get placed in the book hospital (we'll come back to this), but they only get mended and repaired and are allowed to leave the hospital if they pass muster by meeting the remainder of the book audit criteria.

The pile should now consist of books that you *are* familiar with and that are *not* ripped and torn.

Fifth: Time permitting, sit in a cozy chair and read all of the books in the "I am not familiar with" pile and decide if they make the cut. If you don't have time right now, that is OK, but remember, you are not allowed to put these books back on the shelf until you have read them and decided if they make the cut. It might not sound like a super big deal, but let me tell you, I'm not exaggerating when I tell you that sitting down to read an unfamiliar book to children can backfire on you! And in all seriousness, as a professional educator, you have a responsibility to be familiar with all the books you are making available for the children and to select them intentionally, not just because they were on sale or were free. Just because we found a book in the children's section of the library or because someone donated it doesn't mean it deserves a place in your book area.

Sixth: At this point you are going to focus on the pile you have made of the books that are NOT related to any commercialized images, are NOT ripped, have ALL their pages, and that you have read and are familiar with! The final question is this . . . WOULD YOU READ IT TO ME?

Go through and look at the books, skim through them—is it relevant? Is it meaningful? Would you read it to your boyfriend? Your mom? Would you call me on the phone and read it to me? Does it make you say, *OMG! Lisa, I need to read you this book!!!*

And if the answer is no, why are you reading it to the children?

A Few Comments about Donating Books

First, this usually gets people fired up, but it's my opinion and belief all the same. If I won't provide it to the kids in the center, why should it be donated to other kids? The bottom line is crap is crap. If we have determined that it's not fit for the kids *here*, how is it somehow OK for the kids *there*? Second, if I'm trying to spread the word that commercialized books are just that—commercials for shows and products—why would I give them to parents to read to their kids at home? We are sending seriously mixed messages when we do this. Third, do NOT be afraid to throw trash away! You are making room for the high-quality books and stories that *all* children are entitled to!!

Making a Book Hospital

Get a box and spray-paint it white. Paint a Red Cross symbol on each side. If a book gets ripped and there is no time at that moment to fix it, it goes to the hospital and will be scheduled for surgery (repair and mending) at a later date.

Congratulations! You now have a high-quality book center. Let's start reading!

Making Time Each Day to Play

At last we have arrived. The final point within the final point. Making time each day for *play* because when children play they develop social-emotional, language and literacy, cognitive, and physical skills. But even though all four domains are developed during play, and we know the importance of play, the topic of play itself has historically been resistant to research and definition. In 1997 play researcher Brian Sutton-Smith wrote an entire book on the *ambiguity* (having more than one meaning or interpretation) *of play*. Many psychologists and child development theorists have spent considerable time discussing the importance of play as well as attempting to classify the stages and types of play observed in children. I'm talking about as far back as Jean-Jacques Rousseau (1712–1778) and Johan Huizinga (1872–1945) to the theorists I briefly presented a few chapters back, including Montessori, Vygotsky, and Froebel, all the way up to current, contemporary play researchers.

It is no exaggeration that we could spend *the rest of our lives* digging through all the existing papers, books, and articles that summarize, compare, and contrast all of the various theories of play. And as much as I would love to be a part of that extracurricular club, I'm sad to say we don't have time for a full lit review today, guys. (Bummer!) What we *do* have time for is a little bit of history to get the conversation started.

When considering all of the people who have studied and written about children's play, I am going to go out on a limb and guess that the most familiar name for the majority of you is probably going to be Jean Piaget, who identified four stages of play: solitary play, parallel play, associative play, and cooperative play. Sara Smilansky (1922–2006)—who, incidentally, often collaborated with Piaget in her study of play—also identified four stages of play: functional (practice) play, constructive play, games with rules, and dramatic play. She also noted that within these four types of play you might also see evidence of locomotor (physical) play, social play, pretend play, object play, and language play. Mildred Parten (1902–1970) recognized six stages of play in her 1929 doctoral dissertation: unoccupied play, solitary (independent) play, onlooker play, parallel play, associative play, and cooperative play.

Initially these various stages of play were seen as just that, *stages*. Do one, move to the next, then move to the next. More modern, present-day thinking makes room for realizing that children might engage in one *type* of play in one situation and another *type* of play in another, especially if there is a different set of circumstances, such as being in more familiar surroundings, knowing the other children, having previous exposure to the available play materials, and so on. Therefore, in your daily observations of the children in your program, you might see similar types of play among children of *differing* ages and stages, as well as very different types of play between children of the *same* age and stage!

Play Types

I am grateful to Bob Hughes for granting permission to include his list of Play Types in the book for you. Bob Hughes is the director of PlayEducation in the United Kingdom and is a leader on the international playworker scene. He used years of research and observations of children to identify these sixteen types of play.

I believe exploring the Play Types offers many potential benefits:

- It may challenge us to see the depth in what we often simply refer to as *play*.

- It could assist us as we aim to conduct deeper, more relevant observations of children at play.

- It allows us to consider the subtle nuances between various kinds of play.

- It assists us in increasing our vocabulary not only for when we are in conversation with colleagues, but also in our ongoing efforts to boost the credibility of play as a vehicle for playful learning.

- It will encourage us to constantly evaluate the environment to make sure it's ripe for the *child-directed* manifestation of all types of play. I'm going to use this point as a reminder to keep Peter Gray's five characteristics of play in mind as we explore Hughes's Play Types. It's not just about being able to identify the types or committing them to memory, it's about making sure the five characteristics of play are still present—otherwise, it's not play at all.

Here, for your consideration, are Bob Hughes's Play Types listed in alphabetical order. To provide the descriptions of the Play Types, I used my own thoughts as well as two existing summaries of Hughes's work: the "Play Types" information sheet, published by Play Wales, as well as *The Playwork Primer* by Penny Wilson, published by Alliance for Childhood.

My hope is that as you read through the Play Types you think about your children, your students, your friends and consider real-life examples of when you've seen this play in action in your home, life, or school.

COMMUNICATION PLAY

This type of play uses words, jokes, body language, facial expressions, mime, play acting, teasing, whispering, singing (jump rope/hand-clap/playground songs), debate, poetry, graffiti, swearing, emojis, and made-up languages/words/slang or storytelling. Communication Play allows the opportunity for children to practice reading the body language of their peers (such as reading a peer's "play face"), as well as literally playing with language and the spoken word.

CREATIVE PLAY

This is play that allows the expression of the self through any creative medium: clay, paint, glue, music, or even dance. This kind of play is spontaneous yet focused (couldn't we say that of all play??). There is freedom and no planned end result. This is important—while lots of novel, artistic, and open-ended materials might be made available, the focus is forever on the process, not the product! During Creative Play, children have access to a wide range of tools and materials, and, as such, dancing, drama, art, pottery, clay, crafting, gardening, baking, costuming, soap making, jewelry making, glassblowing, and easel painting are all possible examples of Creative Play. Being worried about the mess is NOT a part of Creative Play, nor is having a definitive goal that might distract from the overarching creative process.

DEEP PLAY

When engaged in Deep Play, a child can develop survival skills and conquer fears by engaging in what the *child perceives* to be a risky physical or emotional experience. This is a very important distinction; teachers might not think twice about being barefoot on the grass, yet this could be a huge thing for the child. Deep Play might mean climbing UP the slide or to the top of a tree, scrambling up the jungle gym, walking on a balance beam, maneuvering through an obstacle course, going barefoot, roller-skating, or interacting with snakes, spiders, and other animals the child might be afraid of. This kind of play is very specific to each individual child, so examples would be unique to whatever kinds of experiences that particular *child* perceived as risky, as such, confronting a bully or even playing truth or dare could be examples of Deep Play. This is where observation as well as an understanding of *facilitation* versus *instigation* are very important because it is never our job to push a child just because our environment is tolerant of what might traditionally be classified as "risky" behavior.

DRAMATIC PLAY

In this type of play, children reenact scenes from familiar or recognizable events in which the child was not a direct participant. The Play

Wales "Play Types" document offers that a child was "once removed" from the experience. When children act out TV shows, pretend to be famous rock stars, or act out an event they attended, such as going to a play, parade, concert, or ballgame, it is said to be Dramatic Play. When children prompt other children with questions such as, "Do you want to play *Star Wars*?" they are also engaged in dramatic play. Dramatic Play pulls its plot from a child's wider (remember, "once-removed") experience rather than from personal day-to-day situations (that is more like Role Play and/or Socio-Dramatic Play, but slow down, Sparky! We are going in ABC order!). Dramatic Play scenarios might take place in front of an audience, and the use of makeup, costumes, and elaborate props might be a part of it too.

EXPLORATORY PLAY

This is play where children attempt to *figure things out* by accessing information about a place, area, or *thing* and then, via manipulation or movement, begin to assess its properties and possibilities. Exploratory Play can range from very basic investigations (how does this swing work?) to intermediate ones (how do these Legos stack together?) to more sophisticated examples, such as taking a bicycle or a computer monitor apart and attempting to put it back together. Any play where children might've asked, "What will/might/could happen if _____?" would be examples of Exploratory Play.

FANTASY PLAY

Fantasy Play is pretend play where the child takes full creative license to rearrange the world however he or she sees fit. When children play at being superheroes, aliens, ghosts, pilots of UFOs, or a family of giants that cast spells to save the world from an invasion of bananas that have come to life, they are engaged in Fantasy Play. The difference between Fantasy Play and Dramatic Play is that in Fantasy Play children are playing out scenarios that are unlikely to occur in real life (well, that might depend on who you talk to, but that's another workshop!), and in Dramatic Play children are playing out events that really happened, but, remember, from which they were "once removed." Getting chased by dinosaurs on the playground is Fantasy Play. But if a statement of "Let's play dinosaur!" leads to a group of children pretending to be the dinosaur characters from the movie *Jurassic Park* or *The Land Before Time*, they are engaged in Dramatic Play. It probably goes without saying, but the absence of adults (or at least adults who hover, get too involved, or perhaps even tease or laugh) assists children in engaging in rich Fantasy Play.

IMAGINATIVE PLAY

Play that is based on reality but is not real according to the Play Wales "Play Types" document is Imaginative Play. This is playing *pretend* (this is the key word here) where the child may be acting out scenarios with thematic elements that they may (or may not) have seen or experienced firsthand but that are still based on real things. Pretending to be an elephant, talking to an imaginary friend, hitting a home run in a pretend game of baseball, playing air guitar, and pretending to fly a plane, to be a tree, or to be dead are all examples of Imaginative Play. While both Imaginative and Fantasy Play require the use of a child's imagination, if you wanted to really reduce it to the main difference between the two, one might say that Fantasy Play is rooted in *not-real* and Imaginative Play is rooted in *real, but not for reals*. And just like Fantasy Play, Imaginative Play flourishes when there is minimal adult intrusion.

LOCOMOTOR PLAY

This is play where children are moving in any direction for its own sake and where they experience the possibilities of their own bodies. Running, chasing, climbing, swinging, rolling, jumping, dancing, and playing tag, chase, dodgeball, or hide-and-seek are all examples of Locomotor Play. This is playful, spontaneous large-motor development at its finest! The elimination of recess from many schools here in the US flies smack in the face of this type of play. And you'd think that with our obesity crisis (Which came first? The chicken or the egg?), the importance of this kind of physical play would go without saying.

Mastery Play

This type of play emerges as children attempt to master, control, and manipulate their environment, either physically or emotionally. Whether they are literally in control of their environment or they have the *feeling* of being in control of it, Mastery Play allows children opportunities to demonstrate their competence over elements of the physical space. Lighting fires, digging holes, using a hammer and nail to build a shelter, redirecting a stream, jumping over a river or boulder, learning to ride a bike, and even having a barbeque are a few examples of Mastery Play. Depending on the nature of the specific location (private school? public forest park? community playground? vacant lot?), opportunities for Mastery Play might or might not have their own designated place/area within the area. Don't worry, we're not cultivating arsonists. Mastery Play provides children the opportunity to engage with the natural world and to learn and respect what it is (and is not) capable of. I'd offer that during Mastery Play, children are able to learn the same about themselves.

Object Play

In Object Play, children use their hand-eye coordination to manipulate and examine various objects. The play is with the object itself and whatever it might do or can be, regardless of the object's "proper use." Examining the use or *potential* of a bowl, string, cloth, paintbrush, bubble wrap, spoon, shells, or a cup is Object Play. Turning something over and around, looking inside of something, or shaking an object to see if something comes out are also examples of Object Play. The basic difference between Object Play and Exploratory Play is that during Exploratory Play, a child is assessing the possibilities of a "thing"; in Object Play, they are exploring the thing itself and increasing fine-motor skills at the same time.

Recapitulative Play

Recapitulative Play often emerges when children are outdoors. Playing war, making weapons, building shelters, making fire, and playing at made-up rituals or languages are examples of Recapitulative Play. The general idea with this Play Type is that there are times when playing that children might be spontaneously rehashing our evolutionary history (think "early human" play). Of note: this is the most recently added Play Type, and there still is quite a bit of speculation as to its existence and many unanswered questions as to the origin and necessity of this type of play. Though it is still surrounded by debate (some blog posts choose to not include Recapitulative Play when they write about the Play Types), I offer it here for your consideration since I didn't think it appropriate to leave an officially added Play Type off the list just because folks are still debating and disagreeing over it. While it might be one of the trickier ones to understand or to consider real-life "I-have-seen-that-in-my-classroom" examples of it, that doesn't mean we can't make room for it or facilitate conversations about it.

ROLE PLAY

Playing at exploring ways of being is Role Play. Pretending to drive a bus, iron the clothes, use the telephone, or be a fireman are examples of Role Play. Role Play is when a child imitates people they are familiar with, but it's typically not an accurate representation of the persona the child takes on—for example, pretending to be an overly strict teacher, an extrafrazzled parent, a sugary sweet doctor. The Play Wales "Play Types" document states that during Role Play, a child might morph into an exaggerated, almost caricaturized or stereotyped version of a character (or person) the child is familiar with.

ROUGH-AND-TUMBLE PLAY

This type of play has less to do with fighting and more to do with big-body play that includes touching, tickling, wrestling, and pushing. Some have quipped that while it's referred to as Rough-and-Tumble Play, it isn't very rough and there's not much tumbling. During Rough-and-Tumble Play, children might discover their flexibility and the exhilaration of display (showing off) and, most importantly, learn the social and interpersonal codes for physical conduct. What does this mean? They learn when to back down. There is a slight overlap here with Communication Play as children learn to *read* each other's cues when they're allowed to engage in Rough-and-Tumble Play. Because many adults are uncomfortable with this kind of play, it is often misunderstood and is immediately stopped because of an adult's fear that it will turn into real fighting, which is very unlikely because the number one rule of Rough-and-Tumble Play (whether it's posted on the wall or not) is that it's *consensual*. Think back to Peter Gray's first characteristic of play, it must be freely chosen and YOU CAN QUIT WHEN YOU ARE DONE. Play fighting, wrestling, and chasing where it is obvious that children are unhurt and are enjoying themselves is not "getting them ready" to be violent, it is Rough-and-Tumble Play.

SOCIAL PLAY

Social Play is play where children are interacting with others during which the rules and criteria for social engagement and interaction might be revealed, explored, and amended. Any situation where there is an expectation on all parties to follow rules, customs, or protocols is Social Play, such as board games, starting a club, playground games, or group projects. Even just navigating "center time" at the preschool or "who is who" in the dress-up area might be Social Play. Social Play is probably the most commonly observed Play Type as many of the other identified Play Types, such as Fantasy Play, Recapitulative Play, and Dramatic Play could also be double-classified as examples of Social Play.

SOCIO-DRAMATIC PLAY

Socio-Dramatic Play is the recreating of real scenes from a child's life and typically (but not always) requires two or more players. These scenes can range from the daily mundane rituals that all preschool teachers see regularly in the dress-up/housekeeping area to scenes more typical of a play therapist's office and everything in between. Having dinner, changing the baby's diaper, taking a bath, getting ready for work are all examples of Socio-Dramatic Play. Socio-Dramatic Play might also be of a more intense personal, social, domestic, or *inter*personal nature as children will often use play to act out traumatic events and display (or explore) emotions that might be too scary to express in real life. There is potential for adults to bear witness to various levels of true social drama; whether reenacting a family fight, attending a funeral, going to divorce court, putting the baby to bed, going shopping, or simply setting the table, the child is engaged in Socio-Dramatic Play and there is the potential for it to be emotionally charged.

SYMBOLIC PLAY

Symbolic Play uses one thing to represent another. It starts out rather basic, like a stick being used as sword, a broom as a horse, a bowl as a hat, or a carrot turning into a microphone. It gradually becomes more sophisticated, such as when a child says that the paper (full of scribbles and inventive spelling) is "their name."

Becoming familiar with Hughes's Play Types has allowed me to appreciate the depth of children's play in a whole new way. A few *years* ago, the American Academy of Pediatrics released an article saying that play is important for children and a few *months* ago, they ramped up their language when they released a new report stating that play is *crucial* to the development of young children. There are dozens of professional journals and associations that research and support play, hundreds of books and textbooks, thousands of scholarly papers and anecdotal articles, and tons of blogs that are all in favor of play. So why do we find ourselves still feeling the need to *defend* something that seems to have ample evidence of its inherent value? Wikipedia has a fourteen-page document on *play* with four of these pages being *references* alone, for crying out loud! It's not like we are making this all up! But I bet sometimes when you are talking with people about the value of play they look at you like you are making it up. And this can get exhausting. And insulting. And if we aren't careful, we may reach a point of saying, "Forget it. It's not worth it. I'm done banging my head against the wall."

BREATHE

Come back to the metaphor. The reason for this book is to provide a philosophical orientation (the philosophical attributes of being child centered) to guide us as we frame the foundation (attribute nine, the seven things, the one we are talking about now) that supports the house of higher learning.

In the last few pages we have made a very strong case as to how daily developmentally appropriate opportunities for creating, moving, singing, discussing, observing, and reading (all of which are *play*) strengthen a child's cognitive, language and literacy, physical, and social-emotional development. Thus, we can say that these six things (creating, moving, singing, discussing, observing, and reading) all lead to *learning*.

When we remind ourselves of Peter Gray's five characteristics of play—that play is self-chosen and self-directed, intrinsically motivated, guided by mental rules, imaginative, and conducted in an alert, active, and nonstressed frame of mind—we can accurately state that these same six things (creating, moving, singing, discussing, observing, and reading) can be done *playfully*.

When we consider the various activities we associate with **creating** (gluing, painting, dancing, crafting, cutting), **moving** (running, jumping, spinning, climbing), **singing** (songs, fingerplays, rhymes, chants), **discussing** (communicating, problem solving, describing, negotiating), **observing** (touching, smelling, tasting, seeing, hearing), and **reading** (stories, poems, nursery rhymes, fairy tales), we see they are all opportunities for *playful learning*.

The evidence is strong and sound. Play is the foundation that supports the house.

Conclusion, Wrap-Up, Parting Thoughts, and Taking the Next Step

I'M NOT GOING to lie to you, figuring out how to put closure on this puppy was quite a challenge. There was a part of me that was like, *Just end it, let that last page be it!* But that was "meet the deadline" Lisa. The "I need to extend my deadline" Lisa realized that I was in what felt like the final hours of a two-year road trip and I was just ready to be out of the car, in the house, kicking off my shoes, and tearing off my bra. (How's *that* for a visual!?) And while I was ready to be done, ready to hit "send" and crack open the I-finally-submitted-the-draft celebratory champagne that's been taunting me in the fridge, I knew I needed to step away for a few days to come back and wrap it all up.

My intention this time around was to identify nine philosophical attributes of being child centered and to reinforce that this philosophical orientation must also be grounded in developmentally appropriate practice, strong relationships, and an understanding of the role of playful learning. Without the presence of these three elements, it doesn't matter how much time you spend creating, moving, singing, discussing, observing, reading, or playing, for that matter, or how much free time you provide, how open your schedule might be, how often you go outside, how few (or how many) rules you may have, or how many theorists you can name and discuss. You can't have one without the other. We must pay attention to *all* the variables that make for a strong foundation, not just the fun and easy ones.

I currently see myself as a defender not necessarily of play, *per se*, but of the foundation of preschool. Not preschool as a grade or a developmental stage or a public service, but of the time children get before they head off to whatever *school* is going to look like for them. I am not bold enough to claim to be a defender of childhood, but maybe that's what it comes down to. In my mind's eye I see myself standing tall, smack in between our metaphorical foundation and the first floor of the house, arms outstretched in a strong, protective fashion, making sure that everything that needs to occur here in the foundation is able to unfold and happen without being bulldozed and trampled by inappropriate standards and expectations of a house being built where the cement is still wet.

When it is all said and done, I have no control over the house that will be built. I am not saying that with any judgment as to whether that's good or bad. It's just the truth. Next year is next year is next year, and I have absolutely no control over it. I am not the boss of next year. What I am the boss of is making sure that *this year* is done in a manner that is in the highest and best interest for the children who show up every day, and that means fiercely, repeat that, FIERCELY protecting the play-based, child-centered foundation that will make that house of higher learning as strong as possible.

While writing I was asked if this book would perhaps be considered either a prequel or a sequel to the *Play* book. Interesting question. I think the two books can stand alone, independent of each other, but if I had to suggest an order in which to read them, I'd say read the *Play* book first and this book second. Why? Mostly because the *Play* book paints a general picture of what we need to be doing with children each day (the seven things), and in this book I wanted to explore the philosophical orientation that guides as we do those seven things. Much like the way a child learns, from big to small, from the general to the specific, my first intention is to get the seven things happening in a program (the big picture) and then start fine-tuning the manner in which we are doing them (the minutiae).

Thinking ahead to TAKING THE NEXT STEP, if I were to outline a plan of attack, it might look something like this:

Phase One

1. The initial goal is to make sure that the **seven things** are happening in your program. So your first step is to either read (or reread) the *Play* book and to take the *time* to answer the questions at the end of each chapter.

2. Identify which of the seven things are already evident in your program. Be specific. In your classroom or program, how *exactly* do you witness creating, moving, singing, discussing, observing, reading, and playing occurring on a daily basis? No cheating!

3. Identify which of the seven things are NOT as evident. What would it take to change this? Make a plan (and take the *time*) to figure out how to make sure all seven things start happening on a daily basis; not as a special treat, but on the regular. This might take a bit of time—be patient with your progress, but don't get lazy.

4. Document your observations (read: gather evidence!!) of the seven things occurring on a regular basis. Bonus points if you can link your observations to the four domains within DAP!

5. Sit here for a spell. Yes, we want to keep our momentum, we also want to make sure that everyone (whether it's you, a solo family child care provider, or a child care center staff of ninety-nine people) is confident as we move forward!

Phase Two

1. Reread *this* book. Whaaatt? Yes. Do it.

2. Reflect on how your program currently shows an understanding of the importance of
   a) developmentally appropriate practice (DAP)
   b) relationships
   c) play

   Again, we are going for specifics here. Where's the evidence? How would I *know* you believed in these three things if I showed up one day (unannounced!) to visit your program? What would I see? Hear? Witness?

During this phase you will run each of the seven things (create, move, sing, discuss, observe, read, and play) through the nine philosophical attributes I presented in this book. I am going to walk you through this by asking some questions. This will take time, so continue to be patient! This third phase has the potential to be an ongoing group or individual self-study. It will also assist if and when you find yourself drifting.

Create

If you have been following the plan I have outlined here, we can work from the assumption that opportunities for creating (not just art!) are being offered on a daily basis. Therefore, our next step is to run **create** through the philosophical attributes we explored in the book. This means asking questions like these:

- Do children have enough time to explore or express their creativity?

- How are we providing opportunities for creating outside?

- What are the "rules" here when it comes to creating?

- Am I controlling the environment or the children?

- Where am I on the "need for control" scale when it comes to creating?

- How much control do I need? How much am I willing to release?

- Are we facilitating (or instigating?) creative opportunities?

- When considering creative opportunities, are you asking my three questions: What am I doing? Why am I doing it? Who is it for?

- How familiar are you with modern and historical theorists who studied or wrote about the importance of creating? Who could some of your name-drops be when talking about the importance of creating?

- Do you have access to articles, books, or websites that address the importance of creating?

- Are we providing creative opportunities that meet the children where they are developmentally? Or are they too easy? Too hard?

- How are all of the senses being engaged while the children are engaged in creative expression?

Move

If you have been following the plan I have outlined here, we can work from the assumption that opportunities for moving around (not just recess!) are being offered on a daily basis. Therefore, our next step is to run **move** through the philosophical attributes we explored in the book. This means asking questions like these:

- How much time is provided for children to move their bodies?

- Are there opportunities for moving around both inside and outside?

- What are the "rules" here when it comes to children moving their bodies?

- Am I controlling the environment or the children?

- Where am I on the "need for control" scale when it comes to children's movement?

- How much control do I need? How much am I willing to release?

- How are we facilitating movement opportunities?

- When considering movement opportunities, are you asking my three questions: What am I doing? Why am I doing it? Who is it for?

- How familiar are you with modern and historical theorists who studied or wrote about the importance of movement? Who could some of your name-drops be when talking about the importance of children moving their bodies?

- Do you have access to articles, books, or websites that address the importance of movement?

- Are we providing movement opportunities that meet the children where they are developmentally? Or are they too easy? Too hard?

- Is it possible for all of the senses to be engaged while the children are engaged in movement activities?

Sing

You should see a pattern emerging! If you've followed the plan, we can work from the assumption that singing is happening on a daily basis and not just at circle time! So our next step is to run **sing** through the philosophical attributes we explored in the book. This means asking questions like these:

- How much time do we spend singing and exploring music?

- Are you singing with children both inside and outside?

- What are the "rules" here when it comes to singing and music?

- Am I controlling the environment or the children?

- Where am I on the "need for control" scale when it comes to music and singing?

- How much control do I need? How much am I willing to release?

- How are we facilitating singing and song?

- When considering the songs that you are singing and the music you are playing, are you asking my three questions: What am I doing? Why am I doing it? Who is it for?

- How familiar are you with modern and historical theorists who studied or wrote about the importance of singing and music? Who could some of your name-drops be when talking about the importance of music and song?

- Do you have access to articles, books, or websites that address the importance of singing?

- Are we providing singing and music opportunities that meet the children where they are developmentally? Or are they too easy? Too hard?

- Is it possible for all of the senses to be engaged while the children are singing?

Discuss

I'm guessing you know the drill! But for the sake of consistency, I'll still outline it here for you. By now we should be able to work from the assumption that opportunities for discussing, communicating, and problem solving are happening on a daily basis, and not just when the teacher gives permission! So our next step is to run **discuss** through the philosophical attributes we explored in the book. This means asking questions like these:

- How much time do we spend discussing?

- How is discussing and communicating happening inside and outside?

- What are the "rules" here when it comes to discussing and problem solving?

- Am I controlling the environment or the children?

- Where am I on the "need for control" scale when it comes to discussing?

- How much control do I need? How much am I willing to release?

- How are we facilitating discussions and problem solving? Are we considering the difference between instigating and facilitating when it comes to discussing?

- When considering opportunities for discussing, are you asking my three questions: What am I doing? Why am I doing it? Who is it for?

- How familiar are you with modern and historical theorists who studied or wrote about the importance of discussing, problem solving and communicating? Who could some of your name-drops be when talking about the importance discussing?

- Do you have access to articles, books, or websites that address the importance of discussing?

- How are we making sure our discussions and problem-solving sessions meet the children where they are developmentally? Are we in a hurry to get to resolution? Or are we holding space for them to practice this important skill?

Observe

By now we should be able to work from the assumption that opportunities for observing and using ALL the senses (touch, smell, taste, see, hear) are happening on a daily basis, not just during "My Five Senses" week! So our next step is to run **observe** through the philosophical attributes we explored in the book. This means asking questions like these:

- How much time is spent observing and using ALL our senses?

- Are you observing and using ALL the senses both inside and outside?

- What are the "rules" here when it comes to observing and using all five senses?

- Am I controlling the environment or the children?

- Where am I on the "need for control" scale when it comes to observing?

- How much control do I need? How much am I willing to release?

- How are we facilitating daily opportunities for observation?

- When considering observing and using the senses, are you asking my three questions: What am I doing? Why am I doing it? Who is it for?

- How familiar are you with modern and historical theorists who studied or wrote about the importance of observation and using the senses? Who could some of your name-drops be when talking about the importance of touch, smell, taste, sight, and hearing?

- Do you have access to articles, books, or websites that address the importance of engaging all of the senses and observation?

- Are we providing observation opportunities that meet the children where they are developmentally? Or are they too easy? Too hard?

- Is it possible for all of the senses to be engaged while the children are observing? (This one is a little redundant, but a little extra practice won't hurt!)

Read

Almost done! Again, if you've been following this suggested plan, by now we can assume you are reading on a daily basis—and not just at circle time or before naptime! So our next step is to run **read** through the philosophical attributes we explored in the book. This means asking questions like these:

- How much time do we spend with books and reading?

- Are we bringing books outside?

- What are the "rules" here when it comes to books and reading?

- Am I controlling the environment or the children?

- Where am I on the "need for control" scale when it comes books and reading them?

- How much control do I need? How much am I willing to release?

- How are we facilitating opportunities for books and reading?

- When considering the books and stories we are reading, are you asking my three questions: What am I doing? Why am I doing it? Who is it for?

- How familiar are you with modern and historical theorists who studied or wrote about the importance of books and reading? Who could some of your name-drops be when talking about the importance of reading?

- Do you have access to articles, books, or websites that address the importance of reading?

- Are we providing books and stories that meet the children where they are developmentally? Or are they too easy? Too hard?

- How might it possible for all of the senses to be engaged while the children are reading?

Play

This one has three parts. First, just like the previous six things, if you have been following the plan I have outlined here, we can work from the assumption that children are playing on a daily basis. So your first task is to run what you are calling "play" through Peter Gray's characteristics of play:

1. Is it self-chosen and self-directed? Can the children quit when they are done?

2. Is it intrinsically motivated? Is the emphasis on process or product?

3. Is it guided by mental rules?

4. Is it imaginative?

5. Is it conducted in an alert, active, and nonstressed frame of mind?

Making any and all necessary adjustments is the first order of business. The goal here is to spend time reflecting on whether what you've been calling play really is play.

The second part is to review the definitions of the Play Types as defined by Bob Hughes: communication play, creative play, deep play, dramatic play, exploratory play, fantasy play, imaginative play, locomotor play, mastery play, object play, recapitulative play, role play, rough-

and-tumble play, social play, socio-dramatic play, and symbolic play. Can you recall times when you witnessed any (or all!) of the types while observing children at play? Are you able to share specific examples? Has learning about the play types influenced your work with children at this juncture?

The third part will be to run **play** through the philosophical attributes we explored in the book. This means asking questions like these:

- Do the children have enough time to play?

- What are options for playing while outside?

- What are the "rules" here when it comes to playing?

- Am I controlling the environment or the children?

- Where am I on the "need for control" scale when it comes to playing?

- How much control do I need? How much am I willing to release?

- Am a facilitating or instigating opportunities for play?

- When considering children's play, are you asking my three questions: What am I doing? Why am I doing it? Who is it for?

- How familiar are you with modern and historical theorists who studied or wrote about the value of play? Who could some of your name-drops be when talking about the importance of play?

- Do you have access to articles, books, or websites that address the importance of play?

- Are we providing time for children to play in ways that meet their needs developmentally? Are there some types of play we are more comfortable with than others? Why do you think that is?

- How are all of the senses activated when children play?

 BREATHE

Take a breath! This was a big project!

Whenever you feel overwhelmed, I invite you to come back to the metaphor of the foundation of play supporting the house of academics. We cannot continue being so overly focused on the house that we ignore the variables that makes the foundation stable and strong. In order to make sure the foundation is *rock solid*, I offer what I have presented in this book as a philosophical orientation that will assist us as we create child-centered, play-based early childhood environments where:

- Children are provided long periods of uninterrupted FREE TIME to play and explore

- Children have lots of OUTDOOR time

- Children are able to explore the environment with FEW RESTRICTIONS

- Adults are CONTROLLING THE ENVIRONMENT, not the children

- Adults serve as FACILITATORS within the space

- Adults are able to ARTICULATE the INTENTION behind their words and actions

- Adults are familiar with the key contributions of historical child development THEORISTS

- Adults know the importance of KEEPING IT REAL

- Children are provided time and opportunity to CREATE, MOVE, SING, DISCUSS, OBSERVE, READ AND PLAY (a.k.a. THE SEVEN THINGS) each and every day

You know how to find me if you need me. Go get after it.

Lisa Murphy

References
and Resources

Applied Educational Systems, Inc. 2019. "What Are 21st Century Skills?" Digital Curriculum for CTE & Elective Teachers. www.aeseducation .com/career-readiness/what-are-21st-century-skills.

Armitage, Marc. 2012. "Risky Play Is Not a Category, It's What Children DO." *Child Links* issue 3, 11–14. www.ncn.ie/images/Barnardos _Childlink_Risky_Play.pdf.

———. 2019. The Ugly Side of Loose Parts." Marc Armitage. https://www .marc-armitage.com/blog-archive/the-ugly-side-of-loose-parts_111s56.

Baker, Katherine Read. 1966. *Let's Play Outdoors*. Washington, DC: National Association for the Education of Young Children.

Barker, Jane E., Andrei D. Semenov, Laura Michaelson, Lindsay S. Provan, Hannah R. Snyder, and Yuko Munakata. 2014. "Less-Structured Time in Childrens Daily Lives Predicts Self-Directed Executive Functioning." *Frontiers in Psychology* 5. doi:10.3389/fpsyg.2014.00593.

Beaton, Caroline. 2017. "Top Employers Say Millennials Need These 4 Skills in 2017." *Forbes*. www.forbes.com/sites/carolinebeaton/2017/01 /06/top-employers-say-millennials-need-these-4-skills-in-2017 /#676042997fe4.

Bettelheim, Bruno. 1987. "The Importance of Play." *The Atlantic*. www .theatlantic.com/magazine/archive/1987/03the-importance-of-play /305129.

Bonnay, Steven. 2017. "Is Your Play Risky Enough?" *Hi Mama Early Child-hood Education* (blog). March 13. www.himama.com/blog/is-your-risky -play-risky-enough.

Bristol, Jennifer. 2017. "A Natural Play Revolution: Hello, Dirt and Sticks. Old-fashioned Fun Is Back in Style." *Children & Nature Network* (blog). July 26. www.childrenandnature.org/2017/07/26/a-natural-play -revolution-hello-dirt-and-sticks-old-fashioned-fun-is-back-in-style.

Center on the Developing Child at Harvard University. 2011. "Early Experiences Shape Executive Function." https://developingchild.harvard.edu/resources/building-the-brains-air-traffic-control-system-how-early-experiences-shape-the-development-of-executive-function.

———. 2017. "Executive Function & Self-Regulation." https://developingchild.harvard.edu/science/key-concepts/executive-function.

Colwell, Jennifer. 2015. *Reflective Teaching in Early Education*. "Types of Play." http://reflectiveteaching.co.uk/books-and-resources/reflective-teaching-in-early-education/teaching-for-learning/9.-curriculum/types-of-play.

Copple, Carol, and Sue Bredekamp, eds. 2009. *Developmentally Appropriate Practice in Early Childhood Programs*. 3rd ed. Washington, DC: National Association for the Education of Young Children.

Dimidjian, Victoria Jean, ed. 1992. *Play's Place in Public Education for Young Children*. Washington, DC: National Education Association.

Dishman, Lydia. 2016. "These Are The Biggest Skills That New Graduates Lack." Fast Company. www.fastcompany.com/3059940/these-are-the-biggest-skills-that-new-graduates-lack.

Edwards, Carolyn P., Lella Gandini, and George E. Forman, eds. 2012. *The Hundred Languages of Children: The Reggio Emilia Experience in Transformation*. Santa Barbara, CA: Praeger.

Elkind, David. 2015. *Giants in the Nursery: A Biographical History of Developmentally Appropriate Practice*. St. Paul, MN: Redleaf Press.

Flannigan, Caileigh. 2017. "Bundle Up and Get Outside: Why Kids Should Play in Winter." Community Playthings. www.communityplaythings.com/resources/articles/2017/winter-activities.

Frost, Joe L., Pei-San Brown, John A. Sutterby, and Cassandra D. Thornton. 2004. *The Developmental Benefits of Playgrounds*. Olney, MD: Association for Childhood Education International.

Ginsburg, Kenneth R., and the Committee on Communications, and the Committee on Psychosocial Aspects of Child and Family Health. 2007. "The Importance of Play in Promoting Healthy Child Development and Maintaining Strong Parent-Child Bonds." *Pediatrics* 119 (1): 182–91. https://pediatrics.aappublications.org/content/119/1/182.

Gray, Peter. 2008. "The Value of Play I: The Definition of Play Gives Insights." *Psychology Today*. www.psychologytoday.com/blog/freedom-learn/200811/the-value-play-i-the-definition-play-gives-insights.

———. 2013. "Definitions of Play." *Scholarpedia* 8 (7): 30578. www.scholarpedia.org/article/Definitions_of_Play.

———. 2014. "Risky Play: Why Children Love It and Need It." *Psychology Today.* www.psychologytoday.com/us/blog/freedom-learn/201404/risky-play-why-children-love-it-and-need-it.

———. 2015. *Free to Learn: Why Unleashing the Instinct to Play Will Make Our Children Happier, More Self-Reliant, and Better Students for Life.* New York: Basic Books.

Green, Jarrod. 2017. *I'm OK! Building Resilience Through Physical Play.* St. Paul, MN: Redleaf Press.

Hanscom, Angela J. 2016. *Balanced and Barefoot: How Unrestricted Outdoor Play Makes for Strong, Confident, and Capable Children.* Oakland, CA: New Harbinger Publications.

Hepp, Allyson. 2017. "5 Health Benefits of Kids Playing Outside." Care.com. www.care.com/c/stories/4178/5-health-benefits-of-kids-playing-outside.

Hodgins, Daniel J. 2009. *Boys: Changing the Classroom, Not the Child.* Manchester, MI: Wilderness Adventure Books. www.danieljhodgins.com/books.

———. 2012. *Get over It! Relearning Guidance Practices.* Manchester, MI: Wilderness Adventure Books. www.danieljhodgins.com/books.

Hughes, Bob. 2002. *A Playworker's Taxonomy of Play Types.* 2nd ed. London: Playlink.

Hyder, Tina. 2005. *War, Conflict and Play.* Maidenhead, UK: Open University Press.

IPA/USA. 2019. "The Case for Elementary Recess." www.ipausa.org/recess_pages/the_case_for_elementary_recess.html.

Jalongo, Mary Renck. 1996. "On Behalf of Children: Why Cute Is Still a Four-Letter Word" (editorial). *Early Childhood Education Journal* 24 (2): 67–70.

Jung, Lee Ann, and Dominique Smith. 2018. "Tear Down Your Behavior Chart!" ASCD. www.ascd.org/publications/educational-leadership/sept18/vol76/num01/Tear-Down-Your-Behavior-Chart!.aspx.

Keeler, Rusty. 2008. *Natural Playscapes: Creating Outdoor Play Environments for the Soul.* Redmond, WA: Exchange Press.

Korbey, Holly. 2014. "Let 'Em Out! The Many Benefits of Outdoor Play in Kindergarten." KQED News. www.kqed.org/mindshift/36858/let-em-out-the-many-benefits-of-outdoor-play-in-kindergarten.

Kutska, Ken. 2013. "The Benefits of Risky Play." Playground Professionals. www.playgroundprofessionals.com/play/benefits-risky-play108.

Leichter-Saxby, Morgan. 2017. "Play Types." Play Everything. https://playeverything.wordpress.com/play-and-playwork/play-types.

Louv, Richard. 2013. *Last Child in the Woods: Saving Our Children from Nature-Deficit Disorder*. London: Atlantic Books.

Lund, Danae. 2018. "Top 5 Benefits of Children Playing Outside." Sanford Health News. https://news.sanfordhealth.org/childrens/play-outside.

Manley, Travis. 2015. "Rip Those Behavior Charts off of the Wall and Burn Them." Progressive Preceptors. www.progressivepreceptors.com/blog /rip-those-behavior-charts-off-of-the-wall-and-burn-them.

McCarthy, Claire. 2018. "6 Reasons Children Need to Play Outside." Harvard Health Blog. May 21, 2018. www.health.harvard.edu/blog /6-reasons-children-need-to-play-outside-2018052213880.

Molomot, Lisa (director). 2013. *School's Out: Lessons from a Forest Kindergarten*. Documentary. Bullfrog Films.

Montessori Academy. 2017. "The Importance of Outdoor Play in Winter." https://montessoriacademy.com.au/outdoor-play-in-winter.

Mooney, Carol Garhart. 2000. *Theories of Childhood: An Introduction to Dewey, Montessori, Erikson, Piaget and Vygotsky*. St. Paul, MN: Redleaf Press.

————. 2012. *Swinging Pendulums: Cautionary Tales for Early Childhood Education*. St. Paul, MN: Redleaf Press.

Nicholson, Simon. 1971. "How NOT to Cheat Children: The Theory of Loose Parts." *Landscape Architecture* 62: 30-34. https://media.kaboom .org/docs/documents/pdf/ip/Imagination-Playground-Theory-of-Loose -Parts-Simon-Nicholson.pdf.

Novotney, Amy. 1995. "Getting Back to the Great Outdoors." *PsycEXTRA Dataset*, 2008. doi:10.1037/e531102009-026.

Oxfordshire County Council. "Play Types." www.oxfordshire.gov.uk/cms /sites/default/files/folders/documents/childreneducationandfamilies /educationandlearning/earlyyearschildcare/workinginearlyyears /outofschool/firstclaim/playtypes.pdf.

Penfold, Louisa. 2016. "Simon Nicholson on the Theory of Loose Parts." May 23. https://louisapenfold.com/2016/05/23/simon-nicholson-on -the-theory-of-loose-parts.

Play Wales. 2017. "Play Types." Cardiff, UK: Play Wales. https://issuu .com/playwales/docs/play_types?e=5305098/53885121.

Rivkin, Mary S. 1995. *The Great Outdoors: Restoring Children's Right to Play Outside*. Washington, DC: National Association for the Education of Young Children.

Sandseter, Ellen Beate Hansen. 2011. "Children's Risky Play in Early Childhood Education and Care." ResearchGate. www.researchgate .net/publication/275039981_CHILDREN'S_RISKY_PLAY_IN_EARLY _CHILDHOOD_EDUCATION_AND_CARE.

Sandseter, Ellen Beate Hansen, and Leif Edward Ottesen Kennair. 2011. "Children's Risky Play from an Evolutionary Perspective: The Anti-Phobic Effects of Thrilling Experiences." *Evolutionary Psychology* 9 (2): 257–84. http://journals.sagepub.com/doi/full/10.1177/1474704911009 00212.

Schwartz, Katrina. 2013. "How Free Play Can Define Kids' Success." KQED News. www.kqed.org/mindshift/27124/how-free-play-can-define-kids -success.

Shumaker, Heather. 2016. *It's OK to Go up the Slide: Renegade Rules for Raising Confident and Creative Kids.* New York: Jeremy P. Tarcher/Penguin.

Sutton-Smith, Brian. 2001. *The Ambiguity of Play.* Cambridge, MA: Harvard University Press.

Tomar, David A. 2019 "The Death of Recess in America." *The Quad.* https:// thebestschools.org/magazine/death-of-recess.

Wikipedia. 2019. "Play." https://en.wikipedia.org/wiki/Play.

Wilson, Penny. 2010. *The Playwork Primer.* College Park, MD: Alliance for Childhood.

Williams, David. 2016. "Risky Play: The Balance Between Caution & Hazard." *First Discoverers* (blog). Wesco. June 16. www.firstdiscoverers .co.uk/risky-play-finding-balance.

Yogman, Michael, Andrew Garner, Jeffrey Hutchinson, Kathy Hirsh-Pasek, and Roberta Michnick Golinkoff. 2018. "The Power of Play: A Pediatric Role in Enhancing Development in Young Children." *Pediatrics.* https:// pediatrics.aappublications.org/content/142/3/e20182058.

Zero to Three. 2016. "Help Your Child Develop Early Math Skills." February 25. www.zerotothree.org/resources/299-help-your-child-develop-early -math-skills.